Robert Eden

Some Thoughts on the Inspiration of the Holy Scriptures

Robert Eden

Some Thoughts on the Inspiration of the Holy Scriptures

ISBN/EAN: 9783337183790

Printed in Europe, USA, Canada, Australia, Japan

Cover: Foto ©Lupo / pixelio.de

More available books at www.hansebooks.com

SOME THOUGHTS ON

THE INSPIRATION OF THE HOLY SCRIPTURES

BY ROBERT EDEN M.A.

(LATE FELLOW OF CORPUS CHRISTI COLLEGE OXFORD)
HONORARY CANON OF NORWICH AND VICAR OF WYMONDHAM

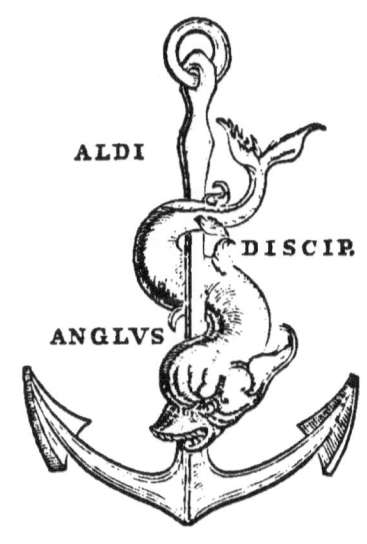

LONDON
BASIL MONTAGU PICKERING
196 PICCADILLY
1864

CONTENTS.

                                    Page

PRELIMINARY . . 1
  Inspiration is acknowledged to be a 'Reality:'
  While there are wide differences of opinion about its Nature.
An intelligent (which alone can be a satisfactory) belief upon the subject is not to be brought about by contrivances.
Disbelief in the authority of Scripture is to be explained upon some broad principles.
We must give to ourselves a 'reason' of our belief: this does not involve the spirit of 'rationalism.'
The Bible has spoken clearly upon the subject of Inspiration.

CHAPTER I.

Revelation and Inspiration . . 27

'Credentials' of the Bible, of all subjects the most interesting:

Of which the 'witness of THE SPIRIT' is the strongest evidence: and, next to this, external considerations.

Nature does not properly 'reveal;' only Historical Facts do this.

Origin of the terms 'Revelation' and 'Inspiration:' the latter expressly Scriptural; ('Theopneustos').

Distinction between the Inspiration of the Writers, and their Writings, groundless.

CHAPTER II.

Ordinary and Special Inspiration 48

The action of the LORD JESUS in 'breathing upon' the Disciples, was significant of 'power from without.'

Inspiration, whether in the sense of 'intelligence,' or of 'personal sanctification,' does not rise up to the idea as it attaches to the Writers of the Books of the Bible:

But it is a question whether the last can be correctly said to differ 'in kind' from the second.

Contents. v

CHAPTER III.

THE MECHANICAL THEORY IS EXPLODED 63

The confused notions on the subject in which men have so long rested, are felt to be unsatisfactory.

The 'organic,' as, indeed, every theory, must be tried upon its own merits.

The Divine and Human elements combine, in Inspiration; but the former predominates.

The illustration drawn from the action upon the strings of a harp, by the player, is just, but may not be pressed too far.

The 'influence' is a preferable term to the 'controul' of the *Spirit*, when His agency in relation to the Scripture Writers is spoken of.

CHAPTER IV.

THE SCRIPTURES WERE COLLECTED BY DIVINE GUIDANCE: AND, THE OLD TESTAMENT IS NOT OUT OF DATE . . 83

The 'collection' of the Books which were to form the rule of the Church's Faith, implied special Divine guidance.

The Old Testament has not done its work, so as to be no longer needed, (the contrary opinion to which may be traced either to philosophical or moral causes);

But is of perpetual use, as appears from its directly *Christian* character,

And because it tells of destinies of the Church yet to be fulfilled.

That 'Scripture' misapplies 'Scripture,' is a charge directly subversive of Inspiration; but is refuted by its own phraseology.

CHAPTER V.

THE SCRIPTURE ASSERTS ITS OWN INSPIRATION 103

The Divine Authority of Scripture is established by external considerations, and is asserted by itself.

St. Paul's language (1 Cor. vii.), furnishes no handle to the notion of intermittent inspiration:

But, on the contrary, strongly supports the other view.

This latter conclusion does not favour the pretensions of 'criticism,' the modern use of which term is illegitimate.

CHAPTER VI.

THE TERM 'SCRIPTURE' IS OF DIVINE ORIGIN AND APPOINTMENT . . 124
A 'commiffion *to write,*' implied either a revelation of new truth, or facts to be recorded.
'Holy,' which is a Scriptural prefix, denotes the dictation of the HOLY SPIRIT, and fo indicates '*authority;*'
A word which is ufed in fenfes which are to be carefully diftinguifhed. As applied to the 'Canon of Scripture,' it declares that the claims of the Books which contain what the Church is to believe, are contained *within themfelves.*
This was the view of thofe who framed the 'Canon,' and is ever to be upheld.

CHAPTER VII.

THE NEW TESTAMENT BEARS WITNESS TO DIVINE "DESIGN" IN THE RECORD OF THE FACTS OF THE OLD . . 144
The ufe of the Old Teftament in the New was *pre-ordained:*

Which implies, alike, the truth, and the inspiration, of the former:
And shews that the latter is not an arbitrary Interpreter.

CHAPTER VIII.

THE QUALIFICATIONS FOR RECORDING GOD'S TRUTH NECESSARILY SUPERNATURAL 151

Free-inquiry is not to be confounded with either Free-thought, or Free-thinking:
The first of which limits itself by the acknowledgment of 'Inspiration,' while the latter two are unrestrained.
Inspiration is supernatural.
To defend THE SUPERNATURAL is the duty to which the Church is at this moment specially called, in opposition to Rationalism:
Which is to be met by boldly maintaining the 'self-evidencing light' of the Scriptures;
And this, as given to the Church generally, and also to the soul of each Believer.
Church-testimony, and our obligations to it, have been greatly exaggerated. Its place and use, as those of Tradition, we admit, provided that the pretensions of each are put forward modestly.

CHAPTER IX.

Inspiration and Human Genius essentially different . . . 190

The 'falfe' meafure of Infpiration is feen when men firft decide of what fort it *ought* to be; the 'true,' when they commence with an *a priori* admiffion of the authority of Scripture to 'decide' that point.

'Infpiration' is neither an intellectual attainment, nor an exalted form of human genius: but, alike in its fource and effects, differs effentially from either.

CHAPTER X.

'Extent' of Inspiration as respects the 'space' 196

The general view of the import of the word 'Prophecy' is very contracted.

A juft view of it, as St. Peter ufes the term, fupplies a moft important argument for the Infpiration of the whole Bible.

A 'Paraphrafe' and 'Comment' will ferve to prefent what is confidered to be the true meaning of St. Peter's words.

CHAPTER XI.

'Extent' of Inspiration, as respects its Quality . . . 213

The essential point in the whole inquiry is, 'In what *sense* do we understand the Scripture Writers to have been inspired?'

The verbal theory cannot be maintained, nor is it required; so that the use of hard names toward those who differ from that view is very blamable.

This theory receives no support from either of three Passages which are often adduced as proving it.

'Grace' and 'Free-will' may be thought to illustrate the case, by analogy.

Some other theories have been held, different from each other, and not all of them in themselves equally objectionable; all, however, inconsistent with the idea of 'full' inspiration.

The Scripture *is*, and does not merely *include*, God's Word. The attempted distinction between 'contains' and 'is co-extensive with,' is not new, but is utterly groundless.

Very important, however, is it to distinguish between the 'essence' contained, and the 'form' which contains it.

Contents. xi

'*All* Scripture is God-breathed,' that is, there is no portion of it which is not.

The Scripture is an infallible interpreter of, and cannot misapply, itself. To assert the contrary, is a flat denial of its inspiration.

Scripture and Science, for their alleged discrepancies, are not to be 'reconciled' by accepting the theory of a "progressive revelation:" in fact, they have never been at variance.

Time can supply evidence in support of Revelation, which, in respect of its Ends, is a perfect Record.

CHAPTER XII.

Some Heads, of Admonition to one class, of Encouragement to another . 260

If any are resolved to close their eyes against Inspiration, they can do so, the proof being essentially and wholly 'moral.'

But candid minds will be convinced of the divinity of the Bible by the unity of its subject, its searching power, its exhaustless resources, and the agreement of its diversified elements.

That 'the evil are mingled with the good,'

in Scripture-hiftory, places no difficulty in the way of belief, fince Infpiration endorfes only the Record, not neceffarily the characters recorded.

The abfence of any exprefs ftatement refpecting Infpiration, from the authoritative ftandards of a Church, proves nothing as to what it holds. Its 'implied' belief is fufficient for all, except merely technical, purpofes.

A revival of belief cannot be looked for, unlefs accompanied by a revival of primitive fimplicity of mind.

Thofe who cannot reafon clofely upon the fubject of Bible-infpiration, may arrive at practical fatisfaction, by looking at the 'effects' of the Scriptures in the world; while All have reafon to be thankful that GOD's meffage to man has come in the enduring form of a 'written' Record.

PRELIMINARY.

ONE of the Writers in a Volume of unenviable fame, after enumerating the chief current explanations of the term 'infpiration,' has this remark:—" All perhaps err in attempting to define what, though real, is incapable of being defined in an exact manner."[1] The admiffion contained in this fentence, coming

---

[1] " On the Interpretation of Scripture," p. 345.

from such a quarter, is very valuable. Inspiration is acknowledged to be a reality.

The same Essayist refers to the distinctions of meaning which the word has received, and asserts that they have been " more numerous than perhaps any other in the whole of theology." This may be true: and if so, it indicates a sense of the importance attaching to the subject itself, for it proves that many minds have been directed to this " reality" to determine its character; just as the variety of views concerning church-organization implies a conviction that government of some sort is essential to the well-being of a religious body; this again, being the expression of a sense of the preciousness of Christian doctrine, since it can be only for the sake of doctrine that the question of order is of any moment. Whence arises this disagreement in opinion about a thing which is 'real?' It must be accounted for by some peculiarity in the form in which it is taught. If there were any such explicit statements of the *nature* of inspiration, as there are sure witnesses of the fact, these would preclude "all strife:" such direct statements, however, are not found.

"Inspiration," says that same Essayist who pronounces it to be 'real,' "is a fact which we infer from the study of Scripture, not of one portion only, but of the whole." Now, just because it is a conclusion drawn from considerations scattered over so wide a field, and in their character so diversified, will the notions respecting it, in ordinary minds, be loose and floating. They who can generalize are the few. To traverse the wide territory of Scripture, and from an almost infinite variety of materials, such as that which is offered by the contents of the Old and New Testament, to seize the features of inspiration, and to make notes of them separately in the mind, so that in their aggregate they shall amount to a full assurance of the Divine authority of the whole record, to such a task as this it is only a few minds that are equal.

Preliminary. 5

Hence the difficulty of framing a definition in which all shall agree, the number of close observers and thinkers, in this case, being necessarily so small. Strong and satisfying as is the evidence that settles down into the soul of him who with candour and devoutness has read the Bible throughout, it is yet made up of particulars for the most part fine and impalpable; or at least, far less capable of becoming the subjects of touch than of feeling. This is, indeed, the peculiarity we should expect to find in a religion which addresses itself mainly to the affections; so far, therefore, is it from being true that the argument for Scriptural inspiration suffers from the lack of evidence capable of being claffed under diftinct heads, that the very genius of the religion of the Bible would feem to make it impoffible that evidence of this fort fhould be afforded.

"The advice" faid to have "been given to the theologian, that he ' fhould take care of words, and leave things to themfelves,'" whether originally defigned to favour "thofe who faid the fame thing and meant another," or not, is, when rightly applied, found. Take care of the words, the chofen terms of the Holy Ghoft; and 'things,' the fubftances of truth of which thofe words are the figns, will be fafe.

"An exceffive importance" cannot be attributed to "the words which the Holy Ghoſt teacheth." The want of a jealous adherence to ſuch words, is the 'error' which has lain at the root of theological as of other confuſions.

But it would be a wrong inference from the fewneſs, or even (were ſuch the caſe) the total abſence of any ſingle definitive abſtract terms in the Scriptures, that there were no 'things' correſpondent to ſuch terms. Single terms gathering up into themſelves the concentrated eſſence of the things to be repreſented, befit and are to be demanded in natural ſcience; but the genius of a revelation from God, given 'in different portions and different manners,' is of another kind. 'The Bible' which, by the very force of the term, we are accustomed to speak of as one book, is really a collection of books quite independent of each other, written at intervals of time, and by various authors; and the very last thing to be looked for in a Volume so composed, would be one or more single terms measuring with precision the degree of guidance by the Spirit which belonged equally to all the books. It is, therefore, to the 'things' we rather look; and so doing, may be safely left to employ the words that shall justly express them. Take a jealous care of 'words,' so far as they are found in or legitimately constructed out of Scripture; and cultivate the same

Preliminary. 9

candour in refpect of 'things,' of fubftances; in other words, of truth: and the refult which may be predicted as regards the prefent fubject is, that Infpiration will be plainly read in Scripture, alike by fingle words and ftatements, and by the impreffion ftamped upon the mind after the ftudy of it as a whole. In this latter refpect it will be analogous to " the obfervance of the Sunday," of which the Author of the *Effay*, " Education of the World," juftly obferves that it[1] " has a *ftronger* hold on the minds of all religious men, *becaufe it penetrates the whole texture* of the Old Teftament."

Infpiration which is 'really' fuch

---

[1] P. 45.

must exclude the idea of essential error. In the narratives there may be, and are variations; but, fundamental discrepancies there are none: so that there is no necessity for referring any differences which are met with, to early " traditions;" a word which takes the thoughts to what is slippery and uncertain; whereas our reliance for the facts of our Lord's history rests either upon eye-witnesses, or upon those who had made the most careful inquiry concerning the facts which they recorded. " An exact fulfilment of prophecy," when its ends are considered, will appear to be a necessary condition to our belief in its inspiration: and so " the absence of such a fulfilment" (could it be made out) would be fatal to its claims as Divine. But the cafe being that we can point to prophecies unqueftionably fulfilled, we fee herein our canons of interpretation confirmed, and that we did not "miftake the letter for the fpirit."

Upheld, however, and vindicated, in each of thofe points of view in which it may have been covertly affailed, Infpiration might at laft be made to yield its ground, if it could be fhown that the " very chiefeft of the Apoftles," for the fupport of the authority of whofe Writings it is mainly afferted, has " hefitated in difficult cafes, and more than once corrected himfelf." In the fame degree, on the contrary, will our belief in infpiration as 'real' be reaffured, if by any arguments it fhall be made to appear that the language ufually alleged as that of 'hefitation' is fimply the reverfe, being the expreffion of an undoubting confidence that, ' he had the Spirit of GOD.'

But when it fhall have been fhown that infpiration is no fiction, but a folid and fubftantial thing; and, when any misftatements or oblique objections fhall have been met by replies, all that is neceffary will not have been done, if there be mifconceptions of its nature. 'Real' in itfelf, and admitted to be fuch, the belief in it may not be real: it cannot be, if it be not intelligent. Now, this end is not to be attained by concessions to the sceptical spirit of the day. An 'intelligent' belief will not be brought about by contrivances to render the subject 'intelligible.'

Upon those Writers who put forth the dogma that "for any of the higher or supernatural views of inspiration there is not any foundation in the Gospels or Epistles," all attempts to present a view of the inspiration-subject that should be admitted as satisfactory, would be thrown away. To these, going the length, as they do, of maintaining that "there is no appearance in their Writings that the Evangelists or Apostles had any" special "inward gift," we can only reply, "Refrain from these men, and let them alone, for, if this counsel or this work be of men, it will come to nought: but if it be of GOD, ye cannot overthrow it, lest haply ye be found even to fight against GOD." GOD help the holders of such opinions: for, with such obliquity of mind it is hopeless to think of coping succesfully.

In passing, however, we would observe that there is yet needed, from the pen of some Christian philosopher, an inquiry into the final causes of those 'departures from the faith' which 'the latter times,' and our own very recent experience, have witnessed. The Publications in which these views are contained have called forth many able replies, in which the misconception of facts, the unfair arguments, and the pofitive ignorance with which, in many inftances, the authors are chargeable, have been expofed. But we wifh for fomething more: we fhould be glad to fee an analyfis of the cafe; to have the original and deeper workings of the minds of the feveral Authors laid open. What is the *root* in the fouls of thofe who have made thefe revolutionary attacks upon the old Faith? An anfwer to this queftion would crown the labours of the feveral Apologifts, by rendering them permanently ufeful.

As a leading element in fuch an inquiry, it will have to be borne in mind, that the affaults upon the authority of the Scriptures, as they have been varied in their character, so have they not been peculiar to one age or country: they have sprung up in different centuries, and different nations. In England, the Deists; in Germany, the Rationalists; in France, the anti-Christian philosophers, have furnished instances of that system of 'free thought,' and 'free handling,' which has acquired the name of 'Neology,' as being altogether *new* and unheard-of in the Church, until introduced in our own Country, (for, its rise was among ourselves, and it went from us to the Continent,) and in those nations. It is, therefore, a phenomenon which has to be accounted for upon some broad universal principles.

Now, just as the human conscience, as such, is the platform on which the Gospel takes its stand, and from which it makes its appeal ("commending ourselves to every man's *conscience* in the sight of God"), so, in the instances, wherever found, of the rejection of God's revealed truth, the human heart, as such, we believe to be the root of the disbelief. Not indeed, that we would impute to the Writers who have themselves so freely used the liberty for which they have pleaded, of "handling the word of God" with freedom, that pravity of heart which would lead them to desire to get rid of the authority of a book whose moral restraints they disliked; (this would be to commit a wanton wrong against high-minded and unimpeachable individuals;) but, the disbelief is that of the heart, or the affections, as it springs out of a strong dislike to entertain the idea of a spiritual Being in close contact with their own spirits, which is just the idea of inspiration as attaching to the Scriptures. How far this resolution to keep the "supernatural" at bay is the silent expression of the thought, " I heard Thy voice, and I was afraid, and I hid myself" (especially since it is often found in company with a " mistaken creed, and the absence of true convictions of sin"), may afford matter for consideration.

Preliminary. 19

But, to offer (as fome have done), as the folution, in all cafes where it is feen, of the fhrinking from the 'fupernatural,' a bad ftate of the perfonal character, would be to inflict a manifeft wrong upon many of the authors of thefe opinions, and to be blind to the marks by which our own day is favourably diftinguifhed from a preceding one in which free fpeculations on religion were put forth in connexion with profane and licentious principles.

"[1] The queftion of the 'final caufe' of the inveftigations which

---

[1] Rev. Prebendary Griffith, M.A., Author of " The Spiritual Life."

are now so eagerly prosecuted, is a deep and wide one. I could not, however, follow some writers in assuming moral delinquency to be at the bottom of it; for I think the present age is honourably distinguished from those of Voltaire and of others, by the spirit in which inquiry puts itself forth, and the honesty and earnestness of purpose which it displays.

"The fact is, that we are in a transition-state; and are exposed to all the evils of such a state. And I confess that I think much of this challenging is due to the extremes of unwarranted assertion to which the Church has been for some years drifting, on the great points of the nature and extent of Biblical authority. And I fondly truſt that the ultimate reſult will be the ſettling down of all Divines into a ſafer, becauſe truer and more juſt theory."

The intereſts of truth as much require that ſatisfactory reaſons ſhould be furniſhed to the reverential thinker for what he is aſked to believe, as that ſufficient replies be made to the cavils of the irreverent ſceptic. If men are to "hold," whether "the Catholic faith," or any other fundamental principles of orthodox Chriſtianity, they muſt be "ready, always, to give a reaſon to" *themſelves* "of the" belief "that is in" them. Any thing ſhort of this is, not indeed neceſſarily diſbelief, but it is unbelief; it is a merely negative condition of mind, whereas faith is pofitive; the 'holding' firmly propofitions offered to its acceptance, from conviction of their truth, upon reafonable evidence. It is not 'rationalifm' to demand a reafon for belief. That term is properly applied to the fyftem which fhuts out miraculous agency, and refufes to admit as true, whatever is not explicable upon natural principles. But, not only has a handle been offered to the fceptic, but hindrances put in the path of honeft believers, by placing fome points of high moment (and of this clafs is the queftion of 'Infpiration'), upon grounds which more careful thought has discovered to be untenable. Suffered, it may be for a very long time, to rest on a foundation thus at last shown to be unsound, the claims of truth, in any one branch of it, suffer damage, not in themselves, but in the eyes of the shallow and superficial, who know not to distinguish between any weak arguments put forth in support of truth, and truth itself. The Church of Christ, too, is injured, by the advantage which its enemies take of the occasion, if ever any one of the props whereon the edifice has rested is thought to have been struck from under it.

"The determination of the limits of what we mean by the inspiration of the Bible" has been pronounced to be one of those studies which must take the lead of all other."

Our 'meaning' is already 'determined' if 'the Bible' have itself spoken with sufficient clearness upon the point. That It has so spoken, not in any sharp definition (for that is not its wont), but unequivocally, it forms a part of our plan to prove.

Most true is it that this 'study' belongs to a class which is entitled to take precedence of all other. It might be added that in that class it stands first. Because it is thus momentous, it is the design of these "Thoughts" to suggest to those who may engage in the study some distinct ideas. Their aim is not to dislodge any positive opinions which may have been "[1] held in unthinking acquiefcence," but to prefent fome views lefs vague than thofe in which even pious and " reverent" minds have been content to reft.

---

[1] Dr. Temple's " Effay," p. 47.

CHAPTER I.

Revelation and Inspiration: the general import of the Terms.

"WRITTEN with the finger of God." This was the authoritative sanction which accompanied the delivery of the two Tables of Testimony, by the LORD, to His minister who was to convey them to the people of Israel. This sanction was, afterwards, appealed to by Moses, when he recapitulated the dealings of GOD with that nation : and, however it may have been practically disregarded by them, at any periods of their history, it has ever been reverentially acknowledged.

Of these Tables copies without number were made for the use of the People; but the original Exemplar was brought from the Mount.

And, "like unto it," analogous to this case of the Decalogue, is that of the entire Scriptures of the Old and New Testament. The channels of conveyance through which the sound has been brought to our ears, have been many and various: but it is as coming "from the excellent glory," that the "voice" commands the attention of the universe of reasonable beings. "Hear, O heavens, and give ear, O Earth, for the LORD hath spoken."

The Divine origin of the Bible is the ground on which every man who holds that book in his hands ultimately rests. If his heart confesses to itself that in the

Revelation and Inspiration. 29

Holy Scriptures it poffeffes a treafure "more precious than rubies," and that to them 'all the things that it can defire are not to be compared,' it is becaufe of the undoubting confidence which is cherifhed that in thofe pages "God hath fpoken." Very far from clear may be the views which any man holds upon the fubject; and farther ftill from precifion the language he employs, if ever he is heard to fpeak of Infpiration: but ftill, there is the belief; deep in his mind, however illogical the habit of it, lies the confidence that the Book has "God for its author;" and only as relying on this as being unqueftionable, does he receive the book as having "truth without any mixture of error for its matter."

Now, to thofe who juftly fet this high value upon the Bible, what inquiry can be fo engaging, what fubject of ftudy fo full of intereft, as that which relates to its credentials? Next to the 'witnefs of the

Spirit,' that private and personal assurance of the divinity of the Scriptures, which, while by the cold sceptic it is, as an argument, rejected, is, by " the honest and good heart," embraced as the strongest argument on which it leans; next to this in worth, every thoughtful person will admit, are all those reasons and considerations drawn from without, by which we can satisfy ourselves that in these books which make up the Volume we thus prize, " GOD has sent Letters to man." " To render a" philosophical "reason" of the matter, to this few will be able to attain; nor, indeed, is this necessary: but, a point will have been gained if some apprehensions of the subject, a little less vague than those generally met with, can be acquired.

There are certain Terms of current use in Theology, which, however familiar to divinity students, require to be explained. Some words have, in popular

Revelation and Inspiration. 31

use, gone away from their original sense: but this ought not to be the case with the terms of theology, nor is it with that subject regarded as a science. Foremost among the words which demand to be thus defined, are "Revelation" and "Inspiration."

In referring to these terms, it would not be possible to invert the order, so as to speak of the latter first, and of the former in the second place; and this, for reasons which will appear as we go on.

Whence comes the word[1] "revelation?" We know that it is from the Latin verb *revelo*, to draw back the veil, to unveil, disclose. Looking at the word

---

[1] In the New Testament ἀποκάλυψις, *Rom.* xvi. 25. (*vide* Koppe on *Eph.* i. 17); a term, says Jerome on *Gal.* i. 12, peculiar to the Scriptures, found in no Greek writer, but invented by the LXX, though used afterwards by Porphyry and Plutarch. The verb (ἀποκαλύπτειν) is common in Classic Greek.

in its ſtructure, it ſuggeſts the act of unveiling; but, its chief uſe in connection with religion is to import the things diſcloſed, the information communicated. 'Revelation' is uſed in theology for the matters revealed.

Among all nations which have, in any degree, emerged out of the ſavage into the civilized ſtate, there are to be found opinions and traditions of a communication between higher beings and men. Often very rudely preſented, the idea is yet found, and that univerſally. All inquiry muſt conduct us to the conviction that the finite "cannot by ſearching find out" the infinite; that " man cannot, by his natural powers, attain to the knowledge of his Maker." For although external Nature makes it plain that " GOD is," and that He acts; for, " the heavens declare ('declarant,' make clear) the glory of GOD," the ſupernatural ſhining forth from the natural: although, too, in the

Revelation and Inspiration. 33

world of thought, our knowledge and our confcience in turn bear witnefs to higher and deeper feelings than could fpring from our own limited faculties; yet thefe are not our difcoveries of GOD, but, fo far as they go, His difcoveries of Himfelf to us. They are "the things which do appear," and conftitute that which "may be known of" GOD, by the ftudy of His outward works, and inward workings; or, as philofophers would precifely exprefs it, by the objective and fubjective evidence HE has given of Himfelf. Now, this is juft what is meant by "Natural Religion," an expreffion which, in our lips, if rightly employed, will ever fignify, not what man eafily arrives at by the exercife of his own faculties, but that which GOD has made known in and by Nature, as comprehending the world without, and the world within us.

Now, none of all this is 'Revelation,' according to the proper intention of that word. It would be incorrect to speak of the sun, moon, and stars, and of the human conscience, as 'revealing' GOD. True "GOD has," in a sense, "spoken" by the phenomena of the universe to the spirit of man, so that "there is no speech nor language" where "their voice" is not "heard," and by those that have ears to hear, heard intelligently; yet it is by facts *historically* conveying to us His "will concerning" us, that a 'Revelation,' in the true sense, is made. It is a great error to contrast natural and revealed religion, (as is sometimes apparently done); but it is equally wrong to confound them. "The mighty GOD, even the LORD, hath spoken and called the earth, from the rising of the sun unto the going down thereof," by a voice that sounds from that very rising and setting. It is, however, "out of Zion, the perfection of beauty," that "the light of the knowledge of the glory of GOD" "hath

Revelation and Inspiration. 35

shined," peculiarly and pre-eminently. Only in the communications He has been pleased to make of himself to the earlier and the later *Church*, whether immediately or by His instruments, has GOD 'revealed' Himself.

For, that great saying, "No man hath seen GOD at any time: the only-begotten Son which is in the bosom of the Father, He hath declared Him," though found in the Gospel, did not begin to be true under the Gospel. Its language points this out; "Who *is* in the bosom of the Father," taking the thoughts at once to the words, "Before Abraham was, I AM;" and announcing the truth, that it is one and the same Divine Being who appeared and spake to Adam, to Abraham, to Moses, and to the Prophets, and who "was made flesh" "for us men, and for our salvation," in the person of "our LORD JESUS CHRIST." The Eternal WORD is the Revealer of GOD, whether "in times past, unto the

Fathers," or " in thefe laft days, unto us." By the agency of none other did GOD declare, though, properly fpeaking, He did not 'reveal' Himfelf in the "things which do appear" of the material world, infomuch that they who liften not to this teaching "are without excufe." "It was the office of the Divine WORD" (says Athanafius), "who, by His peculiar providence and fetting in order of the univerfe, affords inftruction concerning the Father, to renew that fame inftruction." It will be feen that this view goes far beyond the poet's fentiment of admiring praife:

> "The fpacious firmament on high,
>   With all the blue ethereal fky,
>   And fpangled heavens, a fhining frame,
>   Their great Original proclaim:
>
> "The unwearied fun, from day to day,
>   Doth his Creator's power difplay,
>   And publifhes to ev'ry land,
>   The work of an Almighty hand:

with its added comment, when of the moon, stars, and planets, he says:

> "What, though no real voice nor sound
> Amidst their radiant orbs be found;
> In reason's ear they all rejoice,
> And utter forth a glorious voice;
> For ever singing as they shine,
> 'The hand that made us is divine.'"

By all which he can only be understood to convey, that every thoughtful beholder of the celestial system must come to the conclusion, that GOD was its Maker. It maintains that the WORD, as Divine and from eternity creative, and the WORD, as making direct spoken communications to man, is one and the same; the LOGOS, "the manifestative Utterer" of God's will. Yet, it may not be said (simply because it would not be theologically correct to say), that the Creative WORD 'revealed' anything to man: only the WORD speaking did this.

Now, if the revelation made to Adam

and to Abraham and to Moses under the earlier epochs, and in the person of JESUS CHRIST under the later, was not to be lost, it must be preserved by some *record* made of it: in no other way can we conceive of its being transmitted, and becoming perpetual. Does any such document present itself? We know that it does, in a volume existing under the title of 'the Bible,' or, 'the Holy Scriptures.' While the former of these familiar terms suggests the pre-eminence of the record in question, the latter asserts the direct connection of the "Scriptures," of the collective document, with GOD Himself. The attribute "Holy" means this: prefixed to certain writings, it claims for them a special, a proper relationship to the HOLY SPIRIT, as their Author.

And thus we are conducted to the subject of *Inspiration*. Here, too, it is necessary to inquire into the origin of the

Revelation and Inspiration. 39

term. We are familiar with it, frequently uſing it, or hearing it uſed; and we attach ſome ſenſe to it.[1] But whence has it come? The etymology, or derivation of a word will not always determine its ſenſe: it may, and generally will be a help to that end, but it will not always of itſelf fix its meaning; for, a word may have been ſubjected to many influences which affect its ſignification. We cannot always take a word to pieces, and having found its original elements, decide what it does, by arguing what, as ſprung from ſuch and ſuch ſources, it ought to mean.

The word 'inſpiration,' like that already analyſed, comes (we know) from the Latin, that is, immediately; and ſo, regarded in its ſtructure, might, like 'revelation,' deſcribe either the proceſs, or

---

[1] "Uſe and tradition have conſecrated" this word "to expreſs the reverence which all Chriſtians truly feel for the Old and New Teſtaments."— *Eſſay* "On the Interpretation of Scripture," p. 344.

the refult; but, juft as by that word are ufually meant 'the truths revealed,' fo by the term now under confideration is generally intended a quality or characteriftic of the Bible. He who maintains the infpiration of the Scriptures, is by all underftood to teach that the Scriptures are infpired.

But we come back to the queftion, Whence the term? Its elements, we are well aware, are Latin: Spiro, 'to breathe,' in, 'into.' But, as the Latin is not the original language of the Old Teftament, or of the New, we muft fearch yet further. So we fhall find that the warrant for the term 'infpiration,' is contained in a word in the Greek of the New Teftament, which, while it embraces the bafis-element (indeed, effentially the whole) of the term 'infpiration,' includes more, and that a moft important addition. That word is 'GOD-breathed.' So that, while 'infpiration' fpeaks of a 'breathing into,' its original says far more, and pronounces concerning that to which it is attached as the attribute, that it is 'of GOD.' This is not, indeed, the only passage which asserts the Divine original of the Scriptures, but in directness it stands alone, and is to that end so explicit, that if nothing but this were found in the Bible on the point, we should possess, in the words "All Scripture is GOD-breathed," the most ample assurance upon a point of fundamental importance.

For thoughtful and candid minds it were enough to be able to gather satisfaction on this head, indirectly, and by inference: but when it is remembered how many minds are weak and hesitating, not to take into account all that class over which prejudice casts a cloud, it is to be regarded as a momentous advantage, and a ground of thankfulness that we possess a witness so clear, so unqualified, as that which the words now under our thoughts furnish. No student of the Sacred Record, however much his personal conviction may be made up of the 'inward witness' of the Spirit, however true it may be that the evidence which is deepest lodged in his soul, and is there fast riveted, even as the chain which ties the ship to the rock, is the felt adaptation of God's Word to his soul's need; there is no such student but will rejoice in that dogma, standing out like a headland in the sea, sharp, bold, and patent to every eye, "All Scripture is breathed of God."

Such, then, is the origin, such the authority of Scripture. But the very term carries the mind on to the further inquiry, '*Upon whom* breathed?' The reply to which has been already given, in effect, when it was said that God's Revelation could become enduring, for the use of the Church in all future generations, only

Revelation and Inspiration. 43

in one way, namely, by being committed to writing, this neceffarily implying *writers*.

The penmen of the books which compofe the Bible, then, are they into whom God 'breathed' the qualifications, whatever they were, by the exercife of which His will concerning man was to be made known.

It may be thought unneceffary to refer to the ideas held by fome perfons on the fubject of infpiration. Ideas, indeed, they can fcarcely be called; for, judging from the language of by far the greater number of thofe who are ever heard to fpeak on the point, the notions entertained are moft vague, the apprehenfions moft dim. The term 'infpired writers,' as ufed by fuch, expreffes juft what 'facred writers,' or, 'the writers of the Old and New Teftament,' does. As employed by thefe perfons, it merely points to the books, not to any characteriftics which diftinguifhed the writers,[1] or their writings. This is clearly a thoughtless employment of the term, and, therefore, not calling for any notice, except so far as the habit of using words without reflection has a pernicious influence upon the mind, by accustoming it to rest satisfied with faint and general impressions upon subjects in which clearness and precision are all-important, and may be attained. To which ill effects upon the minds of those who allow themselves in the lax use of terms, may be added those which are wrought upon the minds of others who hear and readily acquiesce in those lax statements, through the like indisposition to subject the mind to strict-

---

[1] An undue degree of importance is assigned by some who treat of this subject, beween the inspiration of the *writers*, and the inspiration of the *writings*. Indeed, the distinction itself is one which it is not very easy to apprehend: for it is not of them as 'men,' but as the '*pen*-men' of Holy Scripture that we speak. If, *as* 'writers,' they were inspired, surely so were their 'writings.'

ness in its conceptions; whereby the evil is propagated, and, like a pebble cast into the waters, spreads itself to an almost endless number of circles.

But, turning from this class, if we look at those who do recognise in the term some reference to the condition of the minds of the Writers, the utmost indistinctness will be found to prevail. Seldom is it accompanied by anything beyond a glimpse of the belief that the framers of the contents of the Bible were instructed and guided by GOD, in some sense; but in what sense there seems to be no distinctness of idea. We can imagine some of this sort replying, 'The subject is mysterious.' We admit that it is such in a very high degree, and that the manner of inspiration, *how* it was wrought in the souls of His "servants the Prophets," is of "the secret things" that "belong unto the LORD our GOD." But in this, as in all other matters connected with religious belief, inquiry is not irreverent, nay, is essentially requisite, if our faith is to be intelligent; and unless it be so, it will be "nothing worth," merely negative, rather unbelief than belief. It is not presumptuous to examine into the sense of terms which, if we were to hesitate to employ in respect of things sacred, our hesitation would immediately cause our orthodoxy to be suspected. So that we may lawfully inquire into the meaning of 'inspiration,' as applied to the books which make up the Bible, as there is, unquestionably, no topic in the whole compass of theology which possesses more interest than this. For, if the Scriptures of the Old and New Testament come to us as the charter of our salvation, if we are taught that in them "the GOD of the spirits of all flesh" has spoken to the "reasonable soul" which HE has formed, it is impossible to conceive of any subject that can more delightfully engage our thoughts, than that which relates to the conditions under which thofe "holy men of God," whom in their words and records we believe to have been "moved by the Holy Ghost," did actually 'fpeak,' and write.

CHAPTER II.

Ordinary and Special Inspiration.

WHAT infpiration is effentially, may be regarded as fettled in the term 'God-breathed,' that noble compound, which, as if to keep the Church always right in the main, upon fo vital a point, the HOLY SPIRIT (whofe own proper Name is from the fame ftock) has fupplied, affixing it to the entire Scriptures; for, though it is by the Apoftle applied ftrictly only to the 'Jewifh' Scriptures, we muft fuppofe that he claimed for the Chriftian

Ordinary and Special Inspiration. 49

records no lefs an authority than he conceded to the Hebrew Canon. The Spirit of GOD imprefling, informing the natural faculties, so as to produce a refult diftinct from, and beyond any that could have followed the mere exercife of thofe faculties; that is what we have in our thoughts when we fpeak of the authors of the feveral books that make up the Bible as being 'infpired.' When " the Lord GOD breathed into his noftrils the breath of life, man became a living foul." When HE imparted to the fouls of certain perfons the faculty of recording whether fome new truths which He had communicated to them only, or fome hiftorical facts known to them either by the teftimony or their own eyes, or of others on whom they could rely, there was a Divine communication independent of, and beyond that by which " man became a living foul," peculiar to thofe on whom it was conferred, and fpecial for the ' accomplifhment of the ends for which the agency of thofe men rather than of any other had been felected.

Some help towards a clear perception of this matter we may gain by fixing our attention upon other places of Scripture, with the occafions belonging to them, where the fundamental elements of the word 'infpiration' are found. For, comparifon illuftrates: and we cannot err in comparing the terms "not which man's wifdom teacheth, but which the Holy Ghoft teacheth." Now, we read in St. John, that the Lord JESUS "breathed on them" (the difciples), and faid, "Receive ye the Holy Ghoft," to 'certify them by' that 'fign of His Spirit ever being, not only with,' but *upon and in* them, for the work that lay before them, and to which they were then ordained. Nor may we doubt that, coincidently with that fign, they were "endued with power."

But, it is the meaning of that action

of the LORD as illuſtrative of the point before us with which we are immediately concerned. The natural breath of JESUS was not the Holy Ghoſt, though (as has been ſaid), it may have been accompanied by that Divine gift. Far more important, however, is it to dwell upon that which it unqueſtionably was; a ſign offered to their ſenſes, a token which they ſaw and felt, of *power from without* to " dwell with" them, and to " be in" them, whereby they ſhould be enabled unto all the parts of their work, whether to preach, or act, or write. Carry, now, this thought (of ' breathing-upon' as importing *power*), to the " GOD-breathed" Scriptures, and you are greatly aided in forming an idea of that ' inſpiration' which we claim for the Sacred Writers. " Without" CHRIST, ' apart from' Him and His Spirit, they could " do nothing" as inſtruments for the guiding of the Church " into all truth:" while " through CHRIST," ' who gave them *inward* power,' they could " do all things " demanded by their miffion.

An influence defcending into the human foul, mingling with its natural faculties, and working fome refult which but for that operation from without, could not have been exhibited; this, we conceive, is the effential idea of Infpiration.

This would feem to be the fit place for introducing a caution againft being mifled by two ufes of the word ' infpiration,' which are by no means identical with the fenfe in which it applies to the writers of the books which compofe the Bible. The one inftance is from the Scriptures, the other is from the Englifh Liturgy. In the [1] Book of Job are found the following words: " But there is a fpirit in man, and the infpiration of the Almighty giveth them underftanding." It is evident, from the connection in which thefe words are found, that no more was intended by them, (and therefore that no more can be de-

---
[1] Job xxxii. 8.

Ordinary and Special Inspiration. 53

duced from them), than that the understanding which dwells in the soul of man, and which is to be its guide, is a faculty imparted to it by the Almighty, a direct communication from God. Clearly, then, would it be a misrepresentation of their meaning, were any to contend, from these words, that Inspiration rises no higher than intelligence, and that every reasonable man is inspired.

It would be easy to show how illogical is the process in any such method of arguing, while yet we know that its unsoundness offers no security against its being confidently adopted by some. A warning, therefore, against being misled by it cannot be superfluous, when it is remembered, that the admission of it as valid would amount to a total overthrow of Biblical inspiration, in that peculiar sense in which we have ever been accustomed to think of it.

The other error against which a caution

is needed, is that of suppoſing the inſpiration of which ordinary Chriſtians are the ſubjects, and that of the Scripture-writers, to be the ſame. Neither is this to be treated as a light miſconception: rather is it a very ſerious one, the odds to the authority of the Bible being infinite. GOD's "holy inſpiration that we may think thoſe things that be good," and as the power which is to "cleanſe the thoughts of our hearts, that we may perfectly love HIM, and worthily magnify HIS holy Name," this is indiſpenſable for all, for the loweſt and the higheſt intellect alike; for the moſt unlettered, as for the moſt learned member of the Chriſtian congregation.

But, not even the higheſt meaſure of perſonal ſanctification would, of itſelf, form a qualification for becoming an inſpired penman. We find ſome who were endued "with *ſingular* gifts of the Holy Ghoſt," who were yet not called to the taſk of committing to writing any of thoſe revelations and facts which were to make up the future Canon of Scripture. Very different (if we may judge from some modern speculations on this matter), might have been the course pursued, had it been left to man to select, from the company of them that believed, the persons who should record GOD's Truth. The holiest men would, probably, have been fixed upon as therefore the fittest writers. But the LORD "seeth not as man seeth;" and, besides holiness of heart, there were required, in His unerring judgment, certain endowments of mind, such as HE had implanted in one and not in another, of the true members of the " household of faith." It is easy to conceive that some disciple might be " steadfast and unmoveable" in the faith, and "abounding in the work of the LORD," and yet lack those qualifications of mind, and even of the general character, the possession of which was essential to the task of committing to writing " the word of the LORD." Do we not see how to one man is given swiftness of foot, so that he excels as a runner; to another dexterity of hand, so that he becomes a skilful mechanic; and to a third, ability and aptness of some other and different form; each becoming, by virtue of his distinctive talent, useful in his place; while yet, neither of them should be able to write down the principles of the art, or science, in which he was an adept? And see we not, by analogy, how there might well be eminent goodness and devotedness in some or all of "those men that companied with" the Apostles, "all the time that the Lord Jesus went in and out among" them, while yet there should not be found, in the same men, the endowments that could make them suitable channels for conveying the "mind of Christ" to the Church?

Obvious as such views may be to reflecting minds, they are yet far from being admitted by all arguers on this subject, while from not attending to the distinction which has here been insisted on, the most serious errors have followed. For this reason, it were to have been wished that the same word had not been necessary to denote the extraordinary and the ordinary operation of the Holy Spirit. The latter is truly designated 'inspiration;' so is the former: but, the distinction to be made, in speaking of these two aspects of the Spirit's work, is so important as to have made a different term most desirable, could such have been found. Some writers, indeed, have adopted the word 'theopneustia,' as in itself precise, and also marking the difference in question. But, if it is undesirable to discard an established term, it is the more necessary to define its meaning, and to separate its use in connection with one class of objects, from the sense which it properly bears when applied to another.

Of the remarks which have been made

this is the sum. The Sacred Writers were not fitted for their task, merely by the possession of a high measure of personal holiness: nor were they disqualified by reason of the "weakness of" that "mortal nature" which in common with other men they inherited. Eminent sanctity would not, of itself, bring up a disciple of Christ to the standard of 'theopneustia,' so that he could, out of the resources of a mind "renewed in knowledge after the image of Him that created him," write the word of GOD. The most spiritual Israelite, under the Old Covenant, and the most faithful follower of the LORD JESUS CHRIST, under the New, must remain on this side of the line of demarcation that separates the uninspired from the inspired, unless some new communication shall be made to their minds, of "heavenly things" before unknown, and a special guidance vouchsafed, so as that they might speak and write of the new truths imparted to them after an infallible manner. On the other hand, the prefence of flefhly infirmity would not render them ineligible for becoming the channels through which the purpofes of GOD in JESUS CHRIST fhould be made known to the Church: for then, man could never have been employed at all of that end; for, "there is no man that" is not fubject to "like paffions" with the reft of his race. His devotednefs to the fervice of CHRIST, though an effential prerequifite in his character, did not qualify Paul for preaching "CHRIST's Gofpel," or for writing his great Letter to the Romans, any more than the fervent zeal of Peter, or the affectionate attachment of John to his LORD, qualified the one and the other to compofe the Epiftles they have left to the Church: rather was it a diftinct endowment, conferred on them as it was not on other good men, their fellow-believers, who were not 'called to be Apostles,' and penmen of the Holy Ghost.

And, here, for the sake of marking by one compact term, (as is always convenient where it can be done without injury to truth), the distinction on which we have dwelt, between ordinary and special inspiration, there might be a temptation to adopt the language employed, even by some able writers, and to say, that between the inspiration of Prophets and Apostles, on the one hand, and that of ordinary members of the Church, on the other, the difference is one of *kind*. But is not this to be regarded as an artificial refinement, rather than an authorized distinction? and, does not the Scripture refuse to be so trammelled? When any lay it down as an axiom that the work of the Holy Ghost in the Sacred Writers, 'generically' differed from that of which good men, now, are the subjects, do they not lay themselves open to the charge of too much systematizing, and of travelling beyond the limits which the Holy Ghost Himself has prescribed? Divine truth will not bow to canons of this sort, which may be just in themselves, and are often necessary instruments for coercing human thought when exercised upon "earthly things," but by which the wisdom that hath come forth from the bosom of GOD may not be squared. Is it necessary, can it be thought lawful, to attempt greater precision on this point, than that which the Holy Spirit Himself, by the mouth of the Apostle whom He taught, has used in treating of this very subject? The language employed, in the place referred to, is most express: none more dogmatic can be found in any part of the Writings of the Apostles. The following is offered as a just paraphrase of the passage: 'There are distinctions of endowments, but the same Spirit: and, distinctions of services' (in which these endowments would find the scope for their exercise), 'but the same LORD: and distinctions in the effects wrought; whilst it is the same GOD who worketh these effects in all the possessors of these endowments. But while in all, the SPIRIT manifests Himself as the Author of the effects wrought, He distributes to each person, separately, as He will.'

Upon a point so occult as this (as, indeed, upon some others of the same high and mysterious nature), it were both reverential and safe to keep ourselves within the limits which are indicated by Scripture itself when this subject is treated of in its pages. Unless we do so, ours may be the fault of "intruding into those things which" we have "not seen," and of being 'wise in our own conceits.' Its teaching upon the point before us seems to amount to this: Both those who originally composed, and those who now simply obey, the Bible, are to be thought of as "taught of GOD;" but, each after a different manner.

CHAPTER III.

The Mechanical Theory is Exploded.

HERE is nothing unreason-
able in supposing that GOD
may have endowed certain
men with faculties peculiar
to them, because he would employ them
as instruments for making known His
purposes to mankind. We say '*faculties*,'
for it is clear to every reflecting person
that it is through the powers of the mind
inspiration acts. Another theory, indeed,
long prevailed, (if it was not rather a

confused 'notion' than a clearly-defined theory), that GOD caused certain men whom He selected for that purpose, to write down a number of words which He dictated. With the few who ever stopped to inquire what inspiration meant, there was an "unthinking acquiescence" in that view, which held the ground without any rival almost for ages; while in the lips of the many, the word 'inspiration' merely expressed an inward reverence felt towards the Bible, as possessing a character unlike any other book.

The closer thought, however, which this subject has received, if it has not issued in a general agreement upon all the points it includes, has at least ended in men's minds being thoroughly dissatisfied with those loose opinions which had so long existed. Thus much, at least, is now seen, that to move the hands was not to act upon the mind; whereas the old notion of inspiration began and

The Mechanical Theory Exploded. 65

ended in attributing the former agency to the Divine Author of the Scriptures, the mental faculties of thofe whom He employed being in utter abeyance. Not that a 'doctrine' to this effect was maintained; there was no 'doctrine' at all; but the ideas that floated about upon the fubject, as difcovered by the terms ufed in talking and writing, refolved themfelves into the fancy already alluded to, properly defignated the *mechanical* theory, inafmuch as it prefents man as a 'machine,' and nothing more.

There are, probably, not two minds in the univerfe precifely alike in their conftruction, as there are not two faces alike, although every human countenance is compofed of features phyfically the fame. The difference between one face and another is feen in the proportions of the features, and in the manner in which they are adjufted together. In one, fome features predominate, fome are fubordinate; some stand out, some are subdued: and of this height and depression you shall see modifications carried out through a long series of faces, every one of which might be called beautiful, and claim to hold a place in a gallery of pictures, or of busts. Is not the case such and similar in the world of mind? and, if so, why may it not be true; nay, is it not highly probable that HE who said to Pharaoh, "For this have I raised thee up, for to shew in thee my power," may have, in like manner, raised up, for the express end of making them channels of communication between His own mind and the minds of the whole family of man, certain persons whom He accordingly moulded to that purpose, as the potter fashions the clay in his hands, bringing out by his art vessels of various shapes and capacity, some which are destined to higher uses, being therefore of finer material and more exquisite workmanship?

The Mechanical Theory Exploded. 67

Such a view as this is inconsistent with that which (as has been already said), so long prevailed; rather, however, as a confused notion than a well-defined theory of inspiration, that the Sacred Writers were caused to put down a number of prescribed words and syllables, no other, not any more or any less than those which were appointed for them. By this fancy, which so long held the ground alone and undisputed, man, though employed as the instrument, was wholly passive, his part being purely and merely 'organic,' according to the strict sense of that word, as framed from the Greek original signifying 'a tool.'

This has been the favourite system of many religious minds; or rather, language to this effect is often heard to proceed from persons of that character. We would think and speak honouringly of them for their piety, but must express our dissent from their ideas on this subject. It is their very humility, their defire ever to abafe the creature and to exalt the Creator, that makes them cling to a view which, probably, they have never examined; but, in their defire to uphold the principle that "all things are of GOD," they reprefent Him as irrationally ufing His rational creature.

This idea of infpiration can refer, indeed, for its fanction, to no lefs an authority than the pious and wife 'Hooker;'[1]

---

[1] "They [the Prophets] neither fpake nor wrote any word of their own, but uttered fyllable by fyllable as the Spirit put it in their mouths, no otherwife than the harp or the lute doth give a found according to the difcretion of his hands that holdeth and ftriketh it with fkill."—*Serm.* V. 4., vol. iii. *Works, Oxford,* 1841.

"When fuch illuftrations are applied to men as the agents of the HOLY SPIRIT, we fhould remember that the tone and quality of the note depend as much upon the inftrument itfelf as upon the hand which fweeps over its ftrings."—PROFESSOR LEE's *Donnellan Lectures on Infpiration*, p. 80.

The Mechanical Theory Exploded. 69

but muſt, neverthelefs, be examined upon its own merits. The obvious fault in it is that it feems to teach that GOD did not

---

The excellent and learned Biſhop Jewel, too, went the fame length as Hooker, and even farther: "There is no fentence, no clauſe, no word, no fyllable, no letter, but it is written for thy inftruction."—*A Treatiſe of The Holy Scriptures:* edition 1607, p. 37.

To thefe and other defervedly-high names we owe deference, but not uninquiring fubmiſſion. Indeed, upon the prefent, and all points not determinately laid down in the Word of GOD, we only exerciſe "the liberty wherewith CHRIST hath made us free," when to one who aſks us to what 'fchool' of religious opinion we belong,

("Ac ne forte roges, quo me duce, quo Lare tuter?") we reply,

"*Nullius addiɛtus jurare in verba magiſtri:*" taking good care, however, that our ftate of mind is far from that defcribed in the following line:

"Quo me cunque rapit tempeſtas, deferor hofpes;"
HORACE, *Ep.* 1. i. 14–16.

"*Carried about* with every *wind* of doɛtrine."

"Whatever writers I may refer to," fays Archbiſhop Whately, "whether of fmall or of great reputation, I do not mean to appeal to any as of deciſive *use* the mental faculties of the writers at all, but superseded them, "the human agent contributing no more than the pen of a scribe; in a word, he was the pen,[1] not the penman, of the Spirit."

If this theory be exploded, (for thoughtful minds it never did nor ever can satisfy), it has to be considered in what manner the faculties of the minds of the

---

authority, or to adopt them as *guides.* Some of them may be such as to create more or less of a presumption in favour of their opinions till satisfactorily refuted. Others may supply valuable testimony as to the prevailing opinions in their time, or may suggest arguments which are to be judged of according to their intrinsic weight: but I have learned to 'call no man master upon earth,' and to make a final appeal to nothing but the records of inspiration, and the force of just reasoning."— *Preface to "Essays on some of the Peculiarities of the Christian Religion."*

[1] "The mechanical, or verbal theory, however piously intended, really had the effect of degrading the Sacred Writers almost into automatons."—REV. A. S. FARRAR's *Bampton Lectures.*

The Mechanical Theory Exploded. 71

Sacred Writers were enlisted for the work they had to do. In what way, under what conditions, were they made to execute their allotted task of conveying God's truth to their fellow men? Now, in this it is clear that one of the two elements, the divine and the human, must take the lead. Either the memory and the judgment must go first, and the suggestions of the Divine Spirit be made subordinate to them; or, the latter must precede, the former following in subjection to them. On the first supposition the work is, to all effects, a human production, and its authority to be determined by the worth (at whatever estimated), of the arguments which it contains founded on reason, the confessedly predominating, though not the exclusive element: or, it is a superhuman book, a Volume of authorship properly divine, because it originated in the Divine purpose to make a communication to man, the human mind being the channel through which that truth was to be conveyed. Now, as no one for a moment hesitates to admit that this latter is what he means when he speaks of the '*Word of God*,' so all must acknowledge that the Divine influence must preside, and the human agency be merely its servant and instrument. Still, the human element does work, as truly as the Divine.

We may venture to hint at an analogy to this case, to be seen in the union of the Godhead and the manhood, in the person of the LORD JESUS CHRIST. Every orthodox Christian knows into what a heresy he would be instantly precipitated, were he to suppose, that of the two natures which composed His mysterious Person, the human was the distinguishing one, and that the Divine was 'given by measure unto Him;' 'the right faith' being 'that we believe and confess that' the Divine, which preceded even from

The Mechanical Theory Exploded. 73

eternity, did, for mediatorial ends, aſſume the human, the Eternal Son 'taking the manhood into God,' ſo that the Perſon of Christ was, as touching His Godhead, equal, 'as touching His manhood, inferior to the Father.' And yet we hold that in the manhood of Christ, all the faculties of the human ſoul were in as full exerciſe as they are in any of 'us men' who are merely human, while all were penetrated and infinitely illumined by the "fullneſs of the Godhead" which "dwelt in Him bodily." Does there not ſeem to be a proportion (immeaſurably as the caſes are removed from each other); or, at leaſt, a likeneſs, ſuch a reſemblance as ſerves to illuſtrate the point before us, between the union of the Divine and human natures in the Perſon of Christ, and that of the Divine Spirit and the human faculties, in the caſe of thoſe men whom God called to the work of conveying His truth to mankind? Both elements were present, the supernatural and the natural; but the former presided over and controlled the work of which the latter was to be the instrument. Nor do we only say that so it was: we add, so it must needs have been. Man was to be reached through the medium of his affections: [1] "Speak *thou* with us, and we will hear," said the people to Moses. If any man is to be led to draw near and listen, the speaker must be a man like himself. As he cannot endure the sight of GOD unveiled and direct, so he cannot endure to hear the words of GOD sounding immediately in his ears. Accordingly, the medium can be none other than man, his own fellow being: and if so, then it must be the mind of his fellow that is to speak to his own mind, the faculties being allowed their full play, without any force being employed to urge them forward, or to keep them back. More than this;

---

[1] Exod. xx. 19.

we cannot but suppose that each writer was chosen and sent to the work given him to do, because the native mould of his mind was just that which the Divine mind foresaw would exhibit the truth as God willed that it should be exhibited, the type of mind of each writer having been originally cast by the Infinite Mind itself. Doubtless it was His 'everlasting purpose' to throw the truth which He would make known to man as the 'means of his salvation,' into those forms of thought and expression which belonged characteristically to each of those whom He employed, just because each truth so conceived, and so uttered, would precisely express His will. He who once, in long anticipation, said [1] "of Cyrus, He is my shepherd, and shall perform all my pleasure," had "constantly decreed by His secret counsel," to raise up each of the Evangelists, and of the other New Testa-

---

[1] Isaiah xliv. 28.

ment writers, "when the fulnefs of the time" for their fervices fhould have "come." "Before the foundations of the world were laid," HE faid of them feverally, as of "veffels made to honour," of Matthew and his fellow-hiftorians, and in turn of Paul, and Peter, and John, "He is my fervant, and fhall perform all my pleafure;" fhall conceive, and preach, and write "the word of" My "falvation," as I fhall fill his mind, and move his tongue, and guide his pen.

If it fhall feem to any that an operation fo ftringent as this amounts to that very mechanical agency againft which we have been arguing, let him weigh well the two cafes, and he will probably be brought to fee how wide the difference is between merely employing the lips or the fingers of a man, to fpeak or to write down a certain number of words and fyllables, (dead figns as far as he the utterer or the writer is concerned, however full of life

The Mechanical Theory Exploded. 77

in respect of their author); and, the enlisting of the rational soul of the same man as that which is to command the services of the tongue and the hand. 'Why, there is all the difference in the world,' as we should say in common colloquial phrase. For, think of the steps. The SPIRIT of GOD first fills the mind, informing and elevating it, without making it passive. The mind, conscious of this unusual illapse of the Spirit, and of the special commission implied in it, (for consciousness of both these is an essential condition of inspiration), employs the tongue as its instrument to execute the commanded service to the men of the living generation, by crying in their ears, "Thus saith the LORD;" or else, the activity of the fingers to "take the roll of a book, and write therein" the revelation which had been made to it.

An intelligent, orderly process, this. Not so the other, which asserts that GOD suspends the exercise of the reason of the person HE employs, or, at least, sets it aside for the time; and making His own SPIRIT an immediate agent, moves the tongue or the hand of a man without any concurrence of his own will, whereas, at all other times, and for all other purposes, he is excited to speak or to write by the conscious impulse of his own will. Between the highest degree of constraint which the HOLY SPIRIT can be conceived as exercising upon the tongue and hand *through the mind* of the writer, and upon both *independently* of his mind, the difference is infinite.

Some of the early Christian writers have adopted as illustrative of the operation of the SPIRIT of GOD upon man's spirit, in the matter of inspiration, the action of one who plays "upon a harp or lyre, striking it with the plectrum." An elegant poetical fancy, and, kept within due limits, a just illustration: for there is an analogy. We shall, however, incur danger of being misled if we so follow the illustration as to attribute utter subserviency to the human agent; an error into which we might easily fall by fixing our eye upon the hand that strikes the lyre, and seeing how entirely it commands the strings, without equally remembering that there is a musical note proper to each which cannot but be brought out when smitten by the plectrum. The hand of the musician and the natural sound of the strings go together; nay, he strikes them in order to evoke the proper music of each. Just in this manner, (we hold,) did the SPIRIT of GOD employ the natural faculties, the powers which Himself had implanted, of the several men whom HE chose to write the books of the Bible.

It was with this analogy in his thoughts that Origen writes,[1] "Scripture, as a whole,

---

[1] Matt. v. 9. Tom. iii., p. 441, ed. Ben. Paris, 1733.

is God's perfect and complete inftrument, giving forth to thofe who wifh to learn its one faving mufic, from many notes combined, ftilling and reftraining all ftrivings of the Evil One, as David's mufic calmed the madnefs of Saul."[1]

We may accept this beautiful image,

---

[1] "All fuch illuftrations, no doubt, clearly recognize a relatively paffive ftate in the facred penmen; but they by no means imply that fuch a ftate involved inaction or unconfcioufnefs. On the contrary, the decided manner in which the very writers who have made ufe of the fimilitudes in queftion oppofed the erroneous views as to Prophecy with which they had to contend, proves how fenfibly they felt the diftinction which fubfifts between the vibration of the ftrings of an inftrument of mufic, and the pulfations of the human heart touched and animated by the SPIRIT of GOD. Add to this, the marked omiffion by the Fathers, where adopting the language and the analogies employed by Philo, of any allufion to that fuppreffion of intellectual energy, and of the exercife of reafon which, as we have feen, was fo much infifted upon by the Jewifh philofopher."—PROFESSOR LEE's *Donnellan Lectures on Inspiration*, pp. 80, 81.

The Mechanical Theory Exploded.

and derive much inſtruction from it, if only we are careful to regulate its application. If we preſs the ſimilitude too far, we ſhall be "again entangled" in that theory of *mechanical* inſpiration, about which all who give any ſerious attention to the queſtion are now agreed that it is quite untenable.

In the courſe of this argument, the word 'influence' has been uſed, in ſpeaking of the SPIRIT's working upon the mind of one inſpired. That term was uſed adviſedly, in preference to 'controul,' as denoting the 'flowing' of the mind of GOD 'into' the ſoul of the human inſtrument, as a ſtream comes down from its ſpring-head into a channel prepared to receive it, and along the bed of which it runs; whereas 'controul,' taking the thoughts to the government which a charioteer exerciſes over the horſes which he rules by the reins he holds in his hands, would ſeem to lay the ſtreſs upon the human inftrumentality, and make the mind of man to take the lead in the matter of infpiration; for the power of the horfes is the main agent in the cafe of the chariot, however it is moderated by the fkill of the guide.

CHAPTER IV.

The Scriptures were collected by Divine guidance: And, the Old Testament is not out of date.

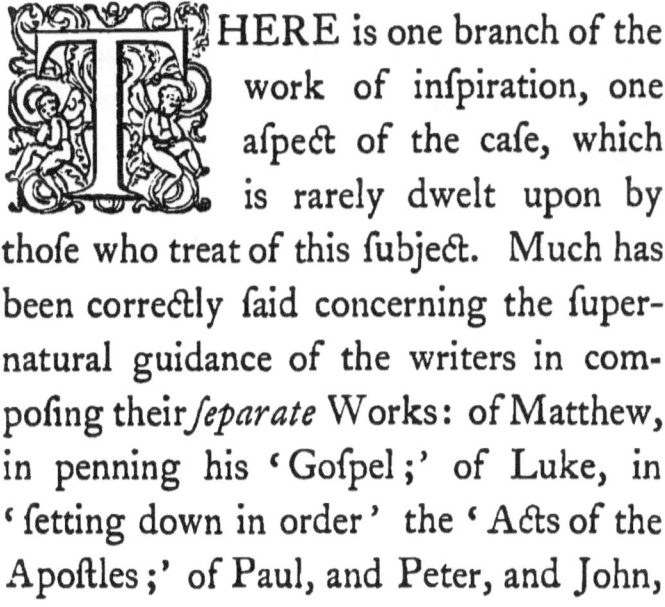HERE is one branch of the work of inspiration, one aspect of the case, which is rarely dwelt upon by those who treat of this subject. Much has been correctly said concerning the supernatural guidance of the writers in composing their *separate* Works: of Matthew, in penning his 'Gospel;' of Luke, in ' setting down in order' the ' Acts of the Apostles ;' of Paul, and Peter, and John,

in compoſing their reſpective Epiſtles. Each, when he had conſtructed his narrative, or penned his apoſtolic Letter, had fulfilled his part. But how were all theſe portions to be brought together, ſo as to form the total of that Truth by which the Church, in the generations to come, was to be taught? There could be no ſpontaneous confluence of theſe ſeveral ſtreams: they could not unite without ſome force from without to bring them together, while only in ſuch union could they become the material of the permanent Faith of the Church. Unleſs, however, this coheſion had been effected, where had been the Faith of the Church? To the inſpiration of the HOLY GHOST muſt be referred this drawing together of the ſingle parts which ſhould make up the whole Canon, the complete rule of the Church of CHRIST; the method employed being the ſame as that by which the ſeparate Books had been compoſed, namely, a faculty divinely imparted of discriminating between the pretensions to inspiration of those authors whose writings were finally admitted into the Canon, and those of any others whose books were rejected. Of this consolidation of the parts, as well as of the composition of each, it may be truly said, "This hath GOD wrought."

But here arises the important question, What was the precise nature of the guidance of those men who collected together the Books which make up the Canon? Was it inspiration of the first, or of the second order; inspiration *proper*, or inspiration *ordinary?* Was it such as dwelt in the writers of the Books, or was it of that sort which some have pronounced to be 'generically' unlike this, although (for reasons already assigned) we have been content to call it 'different,' though, perhaps, not 'in kind'? Now St. John says, towards the end of his Gospel, that " many other signs truly did Jesus in the presence of His disciples, which are not written in this Book: but these are written that ye might believe that JESUS is the CHRIST, the SON of GOD: and that believing, ye might have life through His Name." If it be inquired, Why were "these" (the evidences, probably, of the reality of His resurrection being here particularly intended), "written," and those "other" not: how came it to pass that those were left out of the record, and these included? It is plain: we have it from the Evangelist himself. He passed over certain "signs" which the LORD "did," with, as we must suppose, their attendant discourses and doctrinal comments, such as had accompanied the "sign" vouchsafed to Thomas; while he 'wrote' certain others. By what rule guided, for the insertion and the exclusion? There can be no hesitation in furnishing the reply. That Apostle had "the mind of CHRIST" controlling his own mind, working upon the faculty of judgment, fo as that fome facts he fhould leave out of his narrative, and put in others. If infallibility for choofing and refufing might be found in any, furely it may be looked for in him who was called to be an Apoftle and Evangelift.

But, next to the fpecial direction which was needed for one who, like St. John, was to infert and omit from among the doings of the LORD of the Church, and on whofe infertions and omiffions was to hinge the Faith of the Church to the end of time, fo far as it was dependent upon the document which he compofed; next to this, in order of importance, and demanding a divine difcrimination, was the tafk to which they were called who formed the *collection* of the Books that fhould make up the "Holy" (that is the 'infpired') "Scriptures;" and more particularly, of the Books of the Old Teftament.

In the case of the Books of the New Testament, when their genuineness had been ascertained, all was accomplished that was necessary to make out their claim to a place in the Canon. Let it be a settled point that Matthew was indeed the writer of the narrative which bears his name, and there is no further question to be determined; for the Lord Himself had 'called Matthew from the receipt of custom, to be an Apostle and Evangelist.' Let the authorship of the Epistles to the Romans, Corinthians, and Ephesians, be satisfactorily assigned to St. Paul, and those writings at once take their place as part of the permanent 'Rule' of the Faith of the Church; for an immediate commission from heaven had designated Paul to be the Apostle of the Gentiles. So, too, it may be argued, in respect of each of the remaining historical Books and Letters of the New Testament. Of each the author was either an apostle, or otherwife closely related to the Lord Jesus and His ministry. But the authorship, and therefore the degree of authority attaching to each of the Books of the *Old Testament*, was not so obvious. Believing that the "Pentateuch" bears the stamp of Heaven upon it, and that its credibility as a professed historical record is fully made out, we must yet perceive that the proof of its Mosaic origin is not so immediate as that of the Books of the New Testament. The same is true of the remaining portions of the historical Books of the Old Scriptures. Searching inquiry will conduct us to the same conclusion as they arrived at who first assigned to those writings the rank they hold.

But still it is 'searching inquiry' only that does this: the evidence does not lie upon the surface. So that something beyond common intelligence, something more than mere unassisted acuteness of mind, was necessary to enable them, after spreading open the literature of their own, and of preceding generations, and more particularly those writings which contained the religious element, "to refuse the evil and to choose the good;" to distinguish between the "precious" and the "vile;" to discriminate between "the tares" and "the wheat," gathering the latter into God's storehouse, to be, in combination with the New Testament, the food of the Church for ever.

The faculty which was to judge, from among the books which the world had produced, which contained the Will of GOD, and which did not answer the test, must itself (we say) have been nothing short of 'an' inspiration. Then, of what nature was it? If we adopt the distinction which has been controverted in an earlier part of these remarks, we must assign the collectors of the Books of the Old Testament either to the upper division, making them equal to the Apostles and Evangelifts; or, to the lower, to take their place with ordinary Christians; an alternative which must tend to strengthen our dissatisfaction with that common but, as we venture to think, unwarranted division. Endowments of the SPIRIT, very little short of the highest, were needed for those whose task was to exercise "a right judgment" in such a question.

This divine discernment which qualified the 'Fathers of the primitive age' to repudiate some writings, and to stamp others as entitled to be thenceforward and for ever the 'rule' of what should be believed, this was indeed the "verifying faculty" for which some contend; by which phrase, however (as expounded by the general views of the authors of it), seems to be intended, man's opinion as the tribunal to which that which calls itself inspired is to be brought, to be there tried as to how far it squares with an idea of fitness set up in the human mind, of all things the moſt intangible, and of which no account can be rendered.

The foregoing remarks upon the inſpiration (whatever was its preciſe nature) of thoſe who *collected* the Books of the Old Teſtament, have been prompted by perceiving the growing tendency to diſparage the Old Teſtament, in writers of this day, who ſpeak of it as ſomething out of date, which has done its work, and is now no longer needed by the Church.

The authors of theſe views allege that whatever relates to GOD and to moral duty, having been more completely ſet forth in the New Teſtament than in the Old, the latter has become, as a rule of faith and duty, ſuperfluous. Nay, ſo far have writers of this ſchool gone, as to pronounce " the expreſſions of the nobler and purer heatheniſm " equal to the precepts of the Old Teſtament. The true ſecret of theſe opinions may lie in ſome causes which are kept secret; in some motives which do not appear in the reasons offered by the authors of them. How far they are to be traced to the notion that the whole of the religion inculcated in the Old Testament is of a coarser grain than that taught in the New, and that to make use of it now would be to place ourselves "again in bondage to weak and beggarly elements," or to a dislike of some of the Christian doctrines which acquire force from the significant services of the Jewish ritual, are points worthy of consideration. It is, however, with the fact that we are mainly concerned: that is undeniable, and is to be regarded as one of the worst fruits of modern German criticism.

If we may rapidly glance at the evidence furnished by the New Testament to the perpetual authority of the Old, we cannot but refer, first, to the repeated sanction given by the Lord Jesus to the ancient records, alike in His injunction to "search" them as 'testifying of Himself,' and in the many citations of them in relation to His work. Next, to the assertion made by no less than a Messenger from heaven, and which, though in its strict terms it might seem to be limited to the predictive portion of the Old Testament, to the 'Prophets,' properly so called, must be regarded as really taking in the whole of the Old Testament revelation; predictive intimations of the CHRIST to come being, as we know, found in its very earliest portions; "I am thy fellow-servant, and of thy brethren that have the testimony of JESUS; for the testimony of JESUS is the spirit of prophecy."[1] Of which passage it is to be noted that it is an instance of the transposition of the terms of a proposition, the predicate being here placed before the

---

[1] Revel. xix. 10.

subject; a circumstance, however, which does not alter the real relations of the sentence. On this principle, the proper logical form of the passage is, 'The spirit of prophecy is the testimony of JESUS;' that is, the characteristic sense of prophecy is the witness which it bears to JESUS.

It were endless to multiply proofs from the New Testament, of the point before us. They are so interwoven with its whole texture, that if it should be attempted to dissever and draw them away from the rest, the dissolution of the Record itself would be the consequence. The directly *Christian* character of the writings of the Old Testament, and, therefore, their perpetual use and authority, is taught in those words of St. Paul to Timothy, in which he reminds him of the privilege he had from his earliest days enjoyed, in having " known the Holy Scriptures, which," he says, " are able to make thee wise unto salvation, through faith which is in CHRIST JESUS."[1] For, the juft interpretation of thefe latter words would feem to be, not that an acquaintance with the ancient Scriptures, *fupplemented by* a belief in CHRIST, would favingly enlighten him, but that this bleffed effect was to be looked for in the ufe of them, through belief in CHRIST, to whom "give all the Prophets witnefs."

Forbearing to add here any other confiderations which, were they needed, crowd upon us from the pages of the New Teftament, it may be afked whether it can be imagined, if our LORD enjoined the Jews to "fearch the Scriptures" of the Old Teftament, *becaufe* they teftified of Him, that it fhould have been His defign that fuch a permanent 'witnefs' to Him as "The CHRIST, the SON of the living GOD," fhould be, at any period, withdrawn from His Church? The Old

---

[1] 2 Tim. iii. 15.

Testament must be regarded, not in the light of a scaffolding to a building now complete, but rather as an integral and enduring portion of the edifice itself: 'enduring' (and this constitutes another independent argument for the authority of the Old Scriptures), because containing predictions of events yet to be accomplished, notices of certain destinies of the Christian Church which have yet to be fulfilled; so that those writers who argue as though the Old Testament had done its work, and should now gracefully retire from the scene, proceed upon a false assumption. The Old Testament was, indeed, the messenger which GOD the Father 'sent before the face' of His Son JESUS, to 'prepare His way before Him:' but, unlike the personal forerunner of the LORD, the Hallowed Volume of the Old Covenant was not to "decrease." "[1] The

---

[1] Acts iii. 21.

heavens muft receive" Jesus Christ "until the times of reftitution of all things, which God hath fpoken by the mouth of all his holy prophets fince the world began," are words which declare that there are hidden in futurity (how remote none can fay), events great and organic, in which, when they come to pafs, the Church will recognize what God had fo 'fpoken.' If fo, then muft the Church be looking out for the fulfilment of thefe promifes, with the Volume which contains the "holy prophets," ever open in her hand.

The difpofition to lower the Old Teftament has manifefted itfelf in other forms befide that which has been dwelt on. Of thefe only one can be now mentioned. A diftinction has been drawn between the 'interpretation,' and the 'application,' of Scripture; the former word referring to its 'original meaning,' the latter to the fenfe which certain paffages are made to bear, by those who have employed them.

Now, if the cautions against misinterpretation had been confined to those writers, in our own time, who 'adapt to' their own 'purpose' the words of a Prophet or Evangelist, they might be regarded as wholesome and, perhaps, necessary; for there is a danger of investing with Scriptural sanction those sentiments which are put forth in Scriptural language. A spurious authority may thus be gained for party or private opinions upon any subject.

But, it seems to have been more than hinted by some writers, that *even Scripture itself may misapply Scripture:* nay, that such misapplication is, in fact, found in one place where an Evangelist declares that the words of a Prophet had been " fulfilled " in a recorded event in the infancy of JESUS.

The real question which is raised by

the expression of such opinions is very momentous. It is this. Are we to understand that the use made of the Old Testament in the New is a mere arbitrary and ingenious use? Or, that it is the sense suggested and authorized by that "one Spirit" which dwelt in the writers of both?

We cannot conceal from ourselves that such a mode of arguing as that contained in the criticism referred to, involves a denial of 'inspiration proper' as attaching to the Evangelists; for it represents them as imaginative, fallible, and actually mistaken. Equally plain is it, (did this occur to the author of the criticism now under review?) that if, in one passage, the words of a Prophet so prefaced, may be regarded as employed in a 'conventional' sense, so may they in every other: and that if nothing more than a 'coincidence' could have been 'intended,' the phrase employed is most inappropriate, since the words, "That it might be fulfilled," whether we take them to express a cause, or a consequence, declare unequivocally that the passage cited from the Old Testament received its *full accomplishment* in the fact then being recorded.

The same critics who maintain that "the apprehension of the original meaning of Scripture is inconsistent with the reception of a typical or conventional one," involving (as has been shown), in the charge of such inconsistency, the Sacred Historians themselves, predict the arrival of a "time when educated men will be" unable 'to believe that' certain 'words' which the Evangelist speaks of as "fulfilled" were "*intended*" by the Prophet to refer to the fact in connection with which they are cited. But, the race of new interpreters whose rise is thus predicted, can scarcely surpass in erudition, or power of thought, those men who in past generations, and in our own, have held, concerning the Old Testament, the belief, that it contains many passages which had indeed a positive application to persons or events of the time when they were first uttered, but of which the deeper import was to be understood when brought out in the history of the Gospel Church.

CHAPTER V.

The Scripture asserts its own Inspiration.

PROPOSITION which may surprise many is, that the main argument for the support of Inspiration is to be sought from the Scriptures themselves. " Thou bearest record of Thyself; Thy record is not true,"[1] objected the Jews to our LORD, whose reply is memorable: " Though I bear record of Myself, My record is true." So, and similarly, al-

---

[1] John viii. 13, 14.

though we claim for the Scriptures the right to be heard on behalf of their own divinity, we make no unreasonable demand. It is to be borne in mind that we do not, first, merely hear the voice of Scripture proclaiming its own inspiration, and then call upon all men to submit to its authority without any further inquiry into its pretensions. We do not say, The Bible declares that it is a communication from Heaven, and that the authors of its several Books are " all " immediately " taught of GOD," so that we have now only to receive its doctrines as supernatural revelations, and its histories as unquestionable facts. No such violence as this is attempted to be done against the freedom of our faculties. We assure ourselves, on independent grounds, that the Books are trustworthy: and, then, in the second place, we permit the writers to speak of themselves. The first rank as evidence, is conceded to those arguments by which the Books that are called Holy Scripture are shown to be divine, from considerations external to themselves, those which establish their genuineness and authenticity. These arguments having been heard, and their force admitted, we may fairly and legitimately turn to the record, and ask, "What sayest thou of thyself?" In such a procedure we are not chargeable with the error of 'begging the question;' for, the question of the divine authority of the Scripture has been established upon, we do not say higher but, other and independent grounds: we act modestly, therefore, when we ask that Scripture shall be heard, in the second rank only, asserting its own divinity. It was after HE had wrought miracles, and "done many wonderful works," that our LORD was heard claiming to be acknowledged as having 'come forth from the Father,' and as being 'one' with the 'Father.' Even so, the proofs that the

Books of the Bible were compoſed by their profeſſed authors, and that their contents may be relied upon as true, theſe are, firſt, preſented as the baſis of the pretenſions of the Scriptures; and, "when men have well drunk" at theſe ſprings of conviction, "then" is introduced not "that which is worſe," (on the contrary, it is moſt refreſhing and ſtrengthening), but that which might ſeem gracefully and becomingly, as well as according to philoſophical order, to occupy the ſecond place, namely, the witneſs of Scripture itſelf to its own inſpiration.

Various and multiplied are the forms in which that ſelf-atteſtation is found: none more clear and expreſs than thoſe words of the LORD JESUS, "Search the Scriptures, for in them ye *yourſelves hold*, that ye have eternal life, and they are they which teſtify of Me."[1]

---

[1] John v. 39.

But what, if in the Scriptures themselves shall be found an admission that not every thing they contain is to be regarded as inspired; what shall we then say? Now, it is by no means to be concluded that an objection of this sort must necessarily proceed from a sceptical mind. Candid and reverential readers have thought that they have found reason to adopt views considerably different from what were their former opinions upon the subject of Inspiration, and from the current belief; and this, from the language of Scripture itself. They imagine they find authority for this change, or dissent, in the Apostle Paul's instructions to the Corinthian Church on the subject of marriage.[1] A closer examination, however, of this portion of Scripture than it has received at the hands of many expositors, and of some, it may be, even of those

---

[1] 1 Cor. vii.

whose views of inspiration have become relaxed through the study of this passage in our English version only, may issue in the conviction that it not only lends no countenance to the opinion that the Apostle here admits that he does not speak with authority, as one supernaturally guided, on the point before him, but that it upholds that authority, and exhibits the Apostle as avowing his confident belief that the counsel he offered to the Corinthian Church in their present difficulty was suggested by the Spirit of GOD.

The Apostle, in the place referred to, is drawing a distinction, not between his own private opinion upon the matter in question, and what were his inspired teachings upon other points, whether of doctrine or action; but between his own injunctions as an inspired Apostle, and the command originally given, and which they to whom he wrote well knew to

St. Paul does not hesitate.

have been "given by the LORD." It was an "old commandment" that he would press upon them, not a "new commandment," now, for the first time, issuing from himself. "I speak this *by permission*, and not by way of commandment," is a translation of the words which it would perhaps be presumptuous to pronounce wrong: on the contrary, here, as in not a few other places of the New Testament, we may perceive that the translators rightly apprehended the sense of the original, and expressed in forms of words characteristic of the use of the English language at that day, just what we regard to be the true sense of the passage. The Apostle does not say that he has been permitted but not commanded by the HOLY GHOST, to give this advice; but that this was spoken 'by way of *concession*'[1] (to them in their

---

[1] V. 6. "The preposition κατὰ points out, equally

peculiar trials) and not 'by way of *injunction*.'

But the difficulty seems to rise up with greater force in some subsequent places of the chapter. How are we to explain what is found in the tenth, twelfth, and twenty-fourth verses, to say nothing of the last words of the fortieth? Does not the Apostle, in the two former places, explicitly distinguish between 'inspired' and 'uninspired,' in those verses, respectively: and tell us, in the one in-

---

in both cases, the origin or author of the communications of which he speaks. The directions which he had just given, did not originate with himself. What he wrote was the result of a concession directly made to him? by the Holy Spirit."—*Divine Inspiration.* E. HENDERSON, D.D.; *Lond.* 1847, pp. 280, 281.

In the above passage (from a valuable Treatise), one particular is mis-stated. The 'concession' was not '*made*' to the Apostle: it was made to the Corinthian Christians under their peculiar circumstances; and revealed to the Apostle, who authoritatively communicated it to them. Perhaps the Writer meant this.

stance, that the SPIRIT spake by him, in the other not? The reply is, that it is altogether a gratuitous assumption to make the Apostle refer to the HOLY SPIRIT *speaking in* him. Let those who would rightly apprehend St. Paul's meaning go a little lower, to the twenty-fifth verse, where he says, "I have no commandment of the Lord;" words in which he is not heard to say that he is without any special direction, any inward guidance from CHRIST's Spirit, to give rules for the guidance of the Church, but that there is no definite commandment ever uttered by the LORD JESUS, to which he can refer the Corinthians as an authority upon the matter in question, just as he could not point them to any such as applicable to the other cases. The "not I, but the LORD," of the tenth verse might therefore be thus paraphrased: 'I do not offer, even as an inspired Apostle, my advice: your conduct in this case is determined by a higher authority, by the recorded words of the LORD JESUS, which he spake in the days of his ministry.'

But there is found, in the opinion of some persons, a strong argument against the Apostle's infallibility, in the last words of this chapter, in which he winds up his advice upon the question submitted to him. To the declaration of his "judgment," he adds, " And I think also that I have the Spirit of GOD." So it is in our version: nor is the translation of the original words to be impugned, or to be thought of as inadequately representing the sense. Here, as in some other places where the rendering of the Greek might appear somewhat weak, or even erroneous, it will 'be found upon further consideration' that the translators employed the word or phrase in question, in the sense which criticism would affix to the original expression, and that their Englishing of it fully measures that sense according to the

St. Paul does not hesitate.

import, in their day, of the words they selected, though the use of the words, in our time, be slightly different. For this, however, we appeal confidently to all who have the opportunity of examining the point, that the word employed by the Apostle, and on which objectors fix, is so far from conveying the notion of hesitation, or of a mere 'opinion,' that it is a *firm assertion* that he was divinely guided. 'Now, I *hold*[1] that I, too, have the Spirit

---

[1] A careful examination, in the Original, of the following passages, by creating an assurance that the *very opposite* of a mere opinion is designed in the use, by the sacred writers, of the verb δοκῶ, (to '*hold as a settled view*' of any subject), will fortify the mind against this dangerous suggestion of the enemies of Inspiration. John v. 39, ὑμεῖς δοκεῖτε: '*Your-selves hold*,' &c. Matth. vi. 7. 'They hold' (as a doctrine), &c. Luke xvii. 9. 'No, I hold,' 1 Cor. viii. 2; iii. 18; 'If any one *maintains* that he is wise.' So xiv. 37. and Philipp. iii. 4. Matth. iii. 9. xvii. 25. xxi. 28. xxii. 27. Luke xiii. 2. x. 36. xvi. 2. 1 Cor. iv. 9. x. 12. xii. 23. 2 Cor. xi. 16.

of GOD,' may be regarded as adequately exhibiting the Apoſtle's meaning; which words he is to be underſtood as adding to all that he had written, for the very purpoſe of giving weight to the immediately preceding words, "after my judgment;" and of obviating the ſuppoſition that, in the uſe of that phraſe, he meant to claim no more authority for the advice he had juſt offered, than ſuch as would attach to a private opinion. That he did demand more is evident from the words themſelves, which import much more than the modern colloquial form, ' as *I* think;' or, ' according to *my* view.' For, the Engliſh word " after," as here employed, and agreeably to the principle above laid down, has an emphatic ſenſe. It does not mean, ' if any one is willing to take,' but, ' according to,' ' in purſuance of,'

Galat. ii. 2. δοκοῦσι: 'perſons *thought* much of;' ' *held* in eſtimation;' ii. 9. Heb. xii. 11.

'following,' and, in this sense, '*after*.' 'She is happy if she so abide,' *following therein*, (not 'my *opinion*;' that is not the proper meaning of the term employed, but,) my inspired *decision*; my grave and deliberate *judgment* as an Apostle of Christ, upon the point in question; 'a judgment which' (he had already said, v. 25,) 'I' confidently 'give, not as a private opinion, but as the authoritative counsel of one who has been so graciously dealt with by the Lord, as to be put into the Apostleship, and who thus claims to be *relied upon* in giving a judgment.' 'Now, *I hold* that I, too, as an Apostle[1] of Christ, as one of that number to

---

[1] One of the most satisfying evidences of the Divine Authority of the contents of the 'Epistles,' is the word which meets us in the very outset. "Paul, *an Apostle;*" Peter, *an Apostle* of Jesus Christ." The full credentials of inspiration are here. On whom did the Lord promise to confer the "Spirit of Truth?" Was it not upon the

whom the LORD expressly promised the 'Paracletos' to 'guide' them 'into all truth; though I have distinguished between the original precepts given by the LORD Himself, and my own decisions; I hold that I, too, possess the Spirit of GOD, and am infallibly guided by that Spirit whenever, as now, I write to a Church upon points of faith, or duty, or order.'

It has been thought important to attempt to place this Passage in a right light, inasmuch as both by believers in, and opponents of, Scriptural Inspiration,

---

Apostles? and, for their work? The subject matter of these Epistles was chief among the "many things" which He had to "say unto" them. Therefore the Church, in these Apostolic Letters, possesses the promised supplement to the LORD's personal ministry. It is a necessary conclusion, from the words "an Apostle of JESUS CHRIST" being found prefixed to the several 'Epistles,' that the document, in each instance, at the head of which they stand, is CHRIST's own message to the Church addressed.

by the reverent and the irreverent alike, it is quoted as bearing unfavourably upon that doctrine, against which it presents to the former class, a real difficulty, and furnishes to the latter, a plausible objection.

To have entered thus particularly into the phraseology which runs through this argument will not be deemed superfluous by those who are aware how continually and confidently the Apostle's language, in this place, is referred to as not merely giving[1] support to the opinions of those who are in favour of a relaxed view of inspiration, but as if it contained a direct warning from himself, not to look for Divine authority in all that he delivered. If the remarks upon his words that have now been offered are just, they establish this conclusion, that so far from relinquish-

---

[1] "It furnishes the ordinary burden of all popular reasoning against any strict view of Inspiration."— PROF. LEE'S *Lectures*, p. 291.

ing his claim to be heard as an *inspired* arbiter in the questions he discusses, he asserts such claim in the most decisive manner.

And, here, it may not be out of place to advert to a modern use of the term 'criticism,' which seems quite inadmissible; beneath which, however, some very dangerous speculations have been introduced, and have sought a shield. None will dispute that 'criticism' (as the word has ever, until recently, been understood), is the art of determining the merits of literary compositions: the 'critic' is the person who professes to judge of those pretensions; the 'critique' is the essay which embodies the judgment. But 'criticism,' as such, and properly, has nothing to do with truth and falsehood. He who criticises a composition in verse, refers to some high standard of poetry; he who examines the merits of some popular harangue, tries it by the laws of oratory; such reference to standards implying an admission of the reality of the subjects themselves. The critic remarks upon some particular performance, and points out what he deems to be its beauties and its faults; but his comments are confined to the style and the structure, at any rate to the *circumstances* of the composition, and have properly nothing to do with the subject matter: to examine that belongs wholly to another inquiry. But in our day, and very recently, we have had "free," nay, the very freest "handling" of the *matter* of Holy Scripture, brought before us under the specious title of 'criticism.' The facts upon which the very being of Scripture, as GOD's Truth, depends, are bidden to disappear from the platform of Faith, upon the plea that they cannot abide the canons of a sifting 'criticism.' Let the contents of the "Holy Bible" be subjected to the most searching examination that solid learning can apply; but let not the engine which is really defigned for the deftruction of the City of GOD be brought within its walls under cover of a plaufible title that fhall lull fufpicion, and its falfity be undifcovered, until the moft ferious mifchief has been wrought. No attainment is more to be coveted, no habit more to be cultivated, than of employing, upon every fubject, fuch language as exactly meafures the occafion, fo that we fhall not fay too little, or too much; not felect terms too ftrong, or too weak; above all, not mifreprefent the true nature of the matter on which we fpeak or write. It is, indeed, difficult to conceive how writers poffeffed of fo much keennefs, and who, in the general ftructure of their Works, are characterifed by fingular precifion in the ufe of terms, and feem to have weighed their words with the utmoft nicety, and to have employed them with an aptnefs that agrees with what was to have been

Criticism a perverted term.

anticipated from men of high education, and habits of rigid thought; it is not eafy to underftand how fuch writers fhould have gone fo far away from the fair, the accepted fenfe of any term, as to ufe the word 'criticifm,' as they have throughout, to defignate what is really, and what perfons of their fhrewdnefs could not but have been confcious, was, a deftructive procefs againft the fundamental truths of Holy Scripture, as they have ever been held and received.

This recent and unlawful application of the term in queftion would feem to have crept in through the French. For inftance; there is a Work by an author who ranks under " The Modern School of Free Thought in the Proteftant Church of France," in which are given his peculiar views on Infpiration, the Bible, and Sin, the title of which indicates the nature of the contents, according to the ufe of the word 'critique,' in the original

French; whereas the same word adopted into our English vocabulary, has always been restricted to mean, either a philological inquiry into the meaning of particular words and phrases; or, an examination, generally, into the merits of any work as a literary composition. It must be regarded, therefore, as a dangerous innovation, to use this word freely and repeatedly, when by it nothing less is meant than to raise, in the nineteenth century, the question of the *truth* or *falsehood* (with a plain inclination to a verdict in favour of the latter view,) of those things which for nearly two thousand years "have been most surely believed among us."

If the 'criticism' from which such important consequences to the just 'interpretation of Scripture' are predicted, were soundly applied to the passages which seem to be in the view of those writers who say that the Apostle "hesitated in difficult cases, and more than once corrected himself;" or who, otherwise, make him to have renounced his title to be regarded as inspired, it would, we think, conduct them to a different conclusion. They would discover, that in the word, or words, upon the English rendering of which they found their triumphant 'dictum,' that St. Paul confessed his own fallibility, is contained, not a faint opinion, but on the contrary, a firm assertion of his being inspired; and so, that their anxiety to relieve the Apostle of the burden of " honours thrust upon " him, by pious but weak interpreters of his writings, is superfluous and misplaced.

CHAPTER VI.

The term "Scripture" is of Divine Origin and Appointment.

IT is a point which demands to be borne in mind, as furnishing direct evidence of the divine infallibility of the Sacred Records, that the term by which they are generally known is, *itself*, inspired.

Collectively regarded, the Volume is called " The Bible:" when its several parts, as well as the sum of them, is what is to be described, the term employed is

"The Holy Scriptures." Now, this latter expreſſion is neither a mere Engliſh phraſe, by which we of this nation reverentially deſignate the writings of "holy men of GOD, who ſpake as they were moved by the HOLY GHOST;" nor is it merely a very ancient expreſſion which has come down to us from the times of the Apoſtles, and which might naturally have originated with the Chriſtians of the firſt century ſeeking an appropriate term for the completed Canon. It is far more than this. It is expreſſly of divine origin; and as ſuch, invites our eſpecial attention to its import. The choſen term of the HOLY GHOST poſſeſſes a high degree of intereſt and importance. Now, the phraſe conducts us at once to that which the Bible eſſentially is. 'Scripture' is the *writing-down* of that which had a previous exiſtence, and was to have a permanent uſe. Both theſe elements enter into the idea of 'Scripture.' A revelation had been given, or actions had been done; otherwise there were nothing to place upon record: the revelation and the deeds were of lasting use; otherwise to record them would have been superfluous.

There is found, in the Book of the Prophet [1] Daniel, a passage which illustrates and confirms this view. The angel who instructs him, when referring to certain predictions as being contained in the books he was enabled to "understand," speaks thus: "I will shew thee what is noted in the Scripture of Truth:" remarkable words, first, as being found in the *Old* Testament; and then, as describing a written Prophecy; in which point of view they would seem equally to characterize the predictions of the other prophets. If we place by the side of these words of the divine messenger who spake to Daniel, the first words of the Apocalypse, light will be thrown upon the na-

---
[1] x. 21.

ture of the prophetic writings. St. John declares that he wrote the [1] "record" of [2] "the *revelation* of JESUS CHRIST *which God gave* unto him." In each inftance a 'miniftering fpirit' is the medium of the fupernatural communication; in each the receiver of it *writes down* what he has received; St. John informing us that it was in confequence of repeated inftructions he did fo, and that the angel pronounced, of the entire Record, "Thefe are the true fayings of GOD."

We infer from thefe two parallel cafes, that a 'commiffion to write,' given to men whether of the Old Teftament day, or of the New, implied *a revelation:* in other words, it was juft becaufe fupernatural truth had been conveyed to their minds, that they were to put it into writing, it being [3] "revealed" unto them, "that not unto themfelves, but unto us," to the Church then and onwards, they

---

[1] Rev. i. 1, 2. [2] Rev. xix. 9. [3] 1 Pet. i. 12.

did minister the things miraculously made known to them.

The conclusion in which we rest is simply this; that the word 'Scripture,' as found in the Bible, is a significant term, necessarily implying either a revelation of new truth, or an impulse to place upon record deeds and words, and therein asserting the *inspiration* of the Record itself.

In which conclusion we are confirmed, when passing on to the *New* Testament, we find the same word 'Scripture' continually made use of by the several writers of the historical parts, and by CHRIST Himself, with the addition, in the Epistles, of the remarkable word 'holy,' as a prefix; a word which imports much more than the reverend estimation in which the ancient Scriptures were held, much more than the expression 'hallowed,' (also found); and denoting their character as dictated by the HOLY SPIRIT, with the authority resulting therefrom.

Authority of Canon, Internal. 129

This word *authority*, with the use of which, in its connection with the Holy Scriptures, we are so familiar, requires explanation. For, although not in itself difficult when properly understood, some degree of confusion may attend it to minds not accustomed to look into the strict signification of words; in which sense, of course, they are professedly employed by writers on theological subjects.

In the popular, or at least very frequent use of the word, it conveys the notion of a *demand of obedience*. Thus, a father is said to possess a natural 'authority' over his son; a master exercises the like over his servant; and, generally, those who are lawful governors, over the governed. Of each of these, as being under constitutional rule, an unquestioning submission is demanded.

But it is not exactly in this sense that the word 'authority' is used, in its relation to the Holy Scriptures. They do, indeed, demand to be cordially accepted, and to hold the place of the *rule* of faith and manners to the Church; but this is because they commend themselves to such acceptance by the most powerful considerations. Now, the grounds upon which we of this day receive the Scriptures, and hold ourselves "bound to believe and to do all" that they teach, are precisely the same as those which made them such a law to the early Christian Church; and it is, we conceive, a great error to imagine that we take the Scriptures as our rule, merely because we are historically assured that the first Christians found satisfactory reasons for accepting them as their rule. The Church, in the centuries that succeeded the first, down to this hour, and henceforward as long as its earthly existence shall endure, accepts the Bible as its law, because the reasons which satisfied the

Authority of Canon, Internal. 131

early Christians have convinced, and (it may be presumed), shall ever convince the judgments of each successive generation of Christians.

What, then, were the considerations that prevailed with the early Church to receive the Scriptures? There can be no doubt that it was the *internal* evidence that wrought most powerfully upon the primitive believers. They were not careless, or credulous, as respects the testimony from without. Certain books were, from the very beginning, and by general consent, received among them. [1] All the congregations, or churches, recognized these as divinely given for the use of all, and as *free from error of any kind*, while over some other writings, for a space of

---

[1] "Communi semper conferſu ab omnibus Chriſtianis fuerunt ſuſcepta, et pro canonicis, hoc eſt, Divinis, indubiis, et ad uſum univerſalem Eccleſiarum deſtinatis, nec non omnis erroris in fide et quoad mores expertibus agnita et uſurpata."—WEISMANN. (v. *inf.* p. 134.)

time, hung a degree of doubt; not, however, becaufe they were miftrufted as divine, but only becaufe their authorfhip was not clearly made out. It appears that they were, neverthelefs, read in very many of the churches, and admitted by nearly all, though not as yet formally fanctioned. This hefitation refpecting fome, while others were undoubtingly accepted, is a proof that the Canon of Scripture which has come down to us, was not formed by an eafy acquiefcence on the part of thofe who compofed the early Church; and fhuts out the fufpicion that thofe Chriftians who fixed the faith of Chrift's Church, by fixing its records, were pious, perhaps, but fuperftitious, or eafily fatisfied. [1] It fhews, inconteftably, that they "earneftly" fifted the preten-

---

[1] "All canonical Scripture is infpired; *and becaufe infpired, therefore canonical.*"—"*Teftimonies to the Infpiration of the Holy Scriptures.*" By Rev. A. M'CAUL, D.D., p. 44, Lond. 1862.

sions of that which asked to be a part of the faith that should be "delivered to the saints" of the "generations to come," while, by such cautiousness, they only stamped with a deeper mark of certainty, all those books to which their approving seal stands affixed.

Nevertheless, as has been already said, the main reliance of those Christians rested upon the marks they found *within* the writings, of their contents having 'come forth from God.' Far from overlooking the outer, they yet looked to the inner evidence as their firm footing.

The language of the "Gallican and Westminster Confessions" of the sixteenth and seventeenth centuries, (periods removed by so vast an interval from the time of the Apostles,) in declaring the chief grounds on which the Scriptures were received as divine by the Churches which those Confessions represented, equally expresses the warrant of

134 Inspiration of the Holy Scriptures.

the Church of this century, and of this Nation, for accepting them. In perfect harmony with the sentiments of these 'Confessions,' is the language of a valuable [1] Church Historian, who, when giving an account of the Canon, and of the care shewn by the Christians of the second century in respect of the Holy Scriptures, has this remark, the title of the section being " The *Internal* Unchangeable Authority of the Scriptures." " These writings of the Apostles, which *previously possessed, from God Himself, and His Spirit,*

---

[1] " Autoritas interna immutabilis." "Scripta hæc Apostolica, quæ *jam antea a Deo ipso et Spiritu illius canonicam obtinuerunt autoritatem,* hoc quoque consilio et instituto tradita sunt fidelibus, ut agnoscerentur tanquam γραφαὶ θεόπνευστοι, legerentur ad publicam privatamque institutionem, atque autoritatem in tota Ecclesia Novi Testamenti haberent perpetuam atque universalem, cujus fidei et obsequio nemo se posset subducere."—Weismann's "*Introductio in Memorabilia Ecclesiastica Historiæ Sacræ Nov. Test.*" Halæ. Magdeburg, 1745. (Sect. xxiii. " Historia Canonis Scripturæ.")

a canonical claim to be admitted into the Church, were delivered to believers, with this view, and for this purpofe, that they might be *acknowledged* as Scriptures given by infpiration of GOD, be read for public and private inftruction, and hold, throughout the Church of the New Teftament, an authority which fhould be perpetual and univerfal, from a belief and fubmiffion whereto none might withdraw." Here, then, is the affertion of the original ground on which refted the claim of the Books of the New Teftament to become the rule of faith to the Church: they approved themfelves to the enlightened perception of the Chriftians of that day (many of whom, it is to be borne in mind, had the beft means of knowing what it was the Apoftles had perfonally taught), as being divine. Thofe Chriftians could fay, in the words of the Samaritans, [1] " Now we believe, not

---

[1] John iv. 42.

because of thy saying; for we have heard Him ourselves, and know that this is indeed the Christ, the Saviour of the world:" and we, their successors, to whom has descended the 'deposit' of the Sacred Books, can adopt the same words, as furnishing our answer to any that would inquire of us why we receive those Books. It is a matter of history, open to all, and unquestionable, that at that time, the Scriptures were received upon the *inward* evidence of having been dictated by the HOLY SPIRIT. "So plain is this even from the Sacred Writings themselves," adds the historian above quoted,[1] "and so universally admitted by

---

[1] In another passage, the title of which is, "*There was never any need of a formal Ordinance to prove this authority:*"—"Tam aperta hæc sunt ex ipsis quoque literis sacris, et ab omnibus statim agnita fidelibus, ut nulla synodo, nullis certaminibus aut deliberationibus opus fuerit ad constituendam legem de recipiendis Scripturis; sed reipsa, uno Spiritu

believers from the first, that there was no need of any Synod, of any disputes or debates, in order to set up a law concerning those writings which were to be received; but *by the real teaching of 'One Spirit,'* and with the agreement on all hands of Christians continuing enlightened and true, those Scriptures were accepted as the 'oracles of GOD,' and set forth as binding upon, and for the instruction of all. This kind of Church-tradition we hold as of the highest value, although our belief, in religious matters, rests, *directly and immediately,* upon the truth and word, not of men, but of GOD Himself."

"There be men of cold and icy in-

---

docente, consentientibus undequaque Christianis illuminatis adhuc et veris, ὡς λόγια Θεοῦ fuerint recepta, et ad obligationem ac institutionem omnium proposita. Quod utique traditionis ecclesiasticæ genus maximi æstimamus, etiam si fides Divina non hominum sed Dei ipsius fidei verboque directe et proxime innitatur."—WEISMANN, *eodem loco.*

tellect who must have everything proved unto them." To minds of this order, evidence of the sort just adduced will never be found sufficient; it is moral and internal, while it is of the essence of the habit of such minds to ignore that description of proof. It is better, then, that we should at once profess our belief that the Divine Head of the Church, whilst providing that there should be no lack of authority from without, willed and designed that the deepest and strongest evidence should be that which comes from within the Holy Books. This witness was to the men of the early Church, and is to those of the later, like the Spirit the Author of the records, "a well of water springing up unto" their and our unspeakable, unchangeable conviction. The singular veneration with which those Books were, at the beginning, regarded, and the recognition in them of a character distinct from and above the writings of other "faithful men," must have been so impressed upon the first Christians by the SPIRIT, and therefore by the will of GOD. Very memorable is the saying of Ignatius, in reply to those who strove about some minute matters connected with the mere words of Scripture; and, as he well knew, not from love to the religion of JESUS CHRIST, but out of a spirit of contention against "the truth of the Gospel." "JESUS CHRIST is my '[1] archives;' our uncorrupt cabinet is His cross, and His death, and His resurrection, and the 'faith which is by Him,' whereby I desire, through your prayer, to be justified."

If any one should derive from these words the impression that their author undervalued the written record, or suppose that it was all one to the first Christians whether they used pure or corrupted copies of the Scriptures, or that they

---

[1] Epist. ad Philad. 8.

were in any way careless about the preservation of the text, such an interpreter would go far away from the mind of the writer of that sentiment. His words could never intimate that the Scripture, and CHRIST, and His Spirit, might be independent of each other. Rightly understood, the words of Ignatius are very valuable; they are the profession of one who lived in the very infancy of the Church, that its leading unquestioned facts, as the objective part, and a faith upon CHRIST wrought within the soul, (as it had been in St. Peter's, whose very words, it is to be noted, that Father employs), as the subjective part; that these were the staple, the permanent grounds of the trust of a Christian. Nor is it too much to add, as a corollary, that if we could conceive of the possibility of all the previous documents of the living ministry of the Apostles of CHRIST, and of their Letters to the Churches being

Authority of Canon, Internal. 141

loft, while the history of those facts was preserved, there would be enough left (according to the view of the venerable author of the Epistle to the Church in Philadelphia), for the 'justification' of the soul that should spiritually embrace these few truths.

But besides the care of those first Christians in maintaining the Scriptures, and their estimation of the person and work of CHRIST as the central truths of their faith, which being preserved intact, all that was essential was safe, (the meaning, doubtless, of those words of the ancient Father,) it is certain that the Christians of that early period believed that the Scriptures could become efficacious only by the light and teaching of the HOLY SPIRIT communicated to the souls of believers. If the testimony of antiquity is important and authoritative, let the well-attested convictions of good men, who lived at the very head of the stream, as it issued from the Apostles of Christ, teach us "on whom the ends of the world are come," that an insight into the Scriptures is to be acquired by prayer that the 'door of light may be opened' to us; for that the 'perception' of their true sense is 'given to none but to them to whom God and Christ grant to understand them.' Now, if we candidly listen to the *authority* of antiquity, we shall be found 'earnestly contending for the' same principle. For if it was a true principle then, it is such now, and always, and must be confessed and upheld by Christians of this and of every generation. In the degree, too, in which the spirit that 'exalts above measure,' Reason, as a judge, may depreciate or deny such a rule as this, and refuse, as unphilosophical, to try the inspiration of the Scriptures by the light of the Holy Spirit, on the plea that this doctrine is a part of the system which is upon trial, and, therefore, that such a proceeding would involve the error of a 'petitio principii;' just in that degree to be held in honour are those [1] Writers who have the courage to maintain the obnoxious principle, when they feel that it is not a circumstance merely, nor an appendage, but forms an organic truth of the Gospel 'wherein they stand.'

---

[1] See Rev. E. A. LITTON's valuable work, "Guide to the Study of Holy Scripture:" chap. on "The Interpretation of Scripture:" art. "Teaching of the Holy Spirit." "To understand an author who has been inspired by the Holy Spirit to write, we need ourselves to be under the influence of the same Spirit."

CHAPTER VII.

The New Testament bears witness to Divine " design" in the record of the facts of the Old.

SOME very momentous questions have been agitated of late, having an immediate connection with the matter now under confideration, which is (it will be remembered), Is the Old Teftament, by GOD's appointment, an infeparable portion of the Truth He has left with the Church? To thefe queftions the Scripture fhall furnifh the reply.

"[1]If we attribute to the details of the Mosaic ritual a reference to the New Testament," a dangerous principle has been "conceded." But, then, it is "if *we* attribute to Scripture what it does not itself claim, that this ill consequence will result. Very instructive is a [2]Passage in St. Paul, where he refers to the history of the Israelites in their journeyings, and says twice, that the things which befel them were "ensamples." "*Pre-ordained* types?" or merely such by "accommodation?" an Apostle's accommodation, we know; but, still, such: clever adaptations, and no more?

"[3] Now these things which came to pass, are types *to* us," is the first comment given: and, so far as these words go, no more could be deduced from them than that they are instructive instances. But when, presently, this comment is repeated with an amplification, we are explicitly

---

[1] "Essay," vii. p. 369. [2] 1 Cor. x.
[3] 1 Cor. x. 6.

taught the truth that though facts of the Old covenant days, they are a part of that permanent teaching which GOD has given to the Church under the New Covenant. '[1] Now all these things which befel them are *patterns*' of GOD's retributive dealings with men at all times; 'and they were *made Scripture*, for a warning to us on whom the final dispensations have lighted.'

It is not here asserted that the primary design of GOD in the infliction of these chastisements was to create an example of penal justice; (they did not, in this sense, 'happen unto them for ensamples'): but, that the consequences so befalling those with whom "GOD was displeased," as "the due reward of" their "deeds," became permanent samples of His displeasure against, and His purpose to punish the like sins, always. Nor is it merely

---

[1] 1 Cor. x. 11.

said that from these records of GOD's retributive dealings with Israel, instructive
lessons *may be extracted* by Christians, as
a Statesman reads the past history of nations, and draws from it lessons for his
policy; but, that the things which 'came
to pass' are 'patterns,' model-instances,
to us of the Gospel-day; and that, in
order that they might actually become so,
were by GOD's "determinate counsel"
written and handed down. And thus, the
warning inference, "[1] Let him that *holds*
that he stands" ('trusting in names and
privileges') "take heed lest he fall," is to
be regarded not as the judicious conclusion drawn by Paul, a pious follower of
CHRIST, intelligently reading the early
history of his own nation, but without
"[2] any inward gift," and not "subject to
any power external" to him of an extraordinary kind, but as the great caution of
the Holy Ghost speaking in him, with a

---
[1] 1 Cor. x. 12.   [2] "Essay," vii. p. 345.

view to which use of the history by the future New Testament Church, the prescient mind of GOD, ages before, caused those facts to be written in the 'Book of Exodus,' and elsewhere.

It has been truly urged that "[1] the Old Testament will receive a different meaning, accordingly as it is explained from itself, or from the New." But, it is plain that the explanation of it, (of much of it,) from the New, is not an optional thing; and that the "types and ceremonies of the Law," and (as in the Passage which has been enlarged upon), the "facts of the history," are not "assumed," but very expressly declared to be "after a *pattern*" (under the limitations of the sense which has been assigned to the saying) "corresponding to the things that were to be in the latter days."

The further question stirred by this,

---

[1] "Essay," vii. p. 369.

namely, how we are to regard the interpretation of the Old Teſtament in the New, whether as the "meaning of the original text," or an adaptation of it to the occaſions of later times, does not, ſo put, preſent a fair alternative. Many "types and ceremonies of the law," many facts "and perſons of the hiſtory," had a real, poſitive, and (for the time then being,) perfect meaning; a ſignification and uſe in themſelves. They had, alſo, a "predeſtined" uſe and meaning which was to be brought out in the New Teſtament Day.

In ſome treatiſes which have dealt with this ſubject of "the relation between the Old and New Teſtaments," it is not very eaſy to determine (if, at leaſt, it is forbidden to the reader to ſpeculate upon the 'animus' of many remarks,) whether what is ſaid is levelled againſt New Teſtament commentators upon Old Teſtament hiſtories, or againſt non-Scriptural writers, of whom it was never pretended that they were inspired. A greater degree of clearness in this respect would have saved to readers the pain which is felt, when it is ambiguous whether the "interpreter's fancy," and similar phrases, belong to the Apostles and Evangelists, or to those ingenious mystics who are represented as "having read the Bible crofs-wise."

We are satisfied to rest in the determination which Scripture itself makes of the relation of its earlier and later parts.

These considerations are important far beyond the circle of the particular events to which the Apostle refers. They prove that *the whole record* into the texture of which those histories are wrought, was framed by the will, and under the governance of GOD. Are those alleged actions of the Israelites true? facts, real occurrences? And, admitted to be such, have they been correctly narrated? If we affirm both, then is the 'Pentateuch' itself a history both true and inspired.

CHAPTER VIII.

The Qualifications for recording God's Truth necessarily Supernatural.

THE inspiration theory which, because it represents the authors of the Books of the Bible as simple 'machines' in the hand of the Divine Spirit, has, therefore, been fitly termed the *mechanical*, being discarded, the question will immediately arise in some minds, 'What do you offer in its place?' In a matter, however, so delicate, because so mysterious, the relations involved being those which subsist between the mind of GOD who sends a message, and the mind of man the recipient of it, it is not to be demanded that the place rendered vacant by the dismissal of one theory, should at once be filled up by some other claiming to be free from all possible objection, and complete. So far, indeed, is it from being requisite that one who undertakes to treat of this question, should be prepared with some definite method to make room for which the ground must have been swept clean, that we conceive it to be quite possible that two or more persons may be met with, equally sound in the great fundamental articles of the Christian faith, who yet entertain opinions upon this recondite subject considerably differing from each other. For, it is manifestly impossible, upon a subject so peculiar in its nature, and not expressly treated of in the Record itself, to construct any theory that shall command universal assent. For the 'proof' of the main organic truths of the Catholic faith, we can point to "most certain warrants of Holy Scripture:" but it is otherwise in the present question, so far as respects any one *system*. There is a class of minds to whom it will be a conclusive argument that 'such and such' views were maintained by Chrysostom and Jerome, and by the other Greek and Latin Fathers, as also by the best Divines of the Reformed Church. Doubtless, such information should have the effect of leading students of the Inspiration question to be patient in their inquiries, and modest in announcing their conclusions. But seeing that even those venerable Authorities framed their arguments upon reason and Scripture, it may be permitted to those who enjoy the use of the former, and have lying open before them the page of the latter, to claim the prerogative of Britons, (which they do not forfeit because they are Christians), and to exercise an independent judgment upon this, as upon other topics connected with religious belief: for, to think and to express his thoughts without restraint, is the right of a free-born man.

Freedom of inquiry upon points not settled by inspired authority, is to be distinguished from either 'free-thought,' or 'free-thinking;' the former of which terms expresses the liberty claimed to exercise an uncontrolled judgment upon all subjects, without exception, that can be brought before the mind; while the latter has been (almost technically) employed to mean 'deism,' and came into being in the last century. 'Free-thought' is a wider term, taking in, though not particularizing, religion, an 'improvement' upon 'Free-thinking;' both being euphemisms invented to disguise the objects of each.

There are bounds within which inquirers upon this subject must acknowledge themselves as confined; certain first principles which they are to hold fast, and by which they are themselves to be held. The Advocate for the prosecution, in a recent 'appeal' in the matter of a well-known Volume, was reported as declining to be driven into a metaphysical discussion of the doctrine of inspiration; but contended that it was an influence which conferred upon the books in which it existed, "a certain character different from all other books." He declined, also, to enter into questions of historical truth, or geographical discovery, or scientific accuracy, considering it sufficient for his purpose to point out that the greatest latitude of criticism was allowed to clergymen of the Church of England, limited only by the presence of inspiration, as has been described. He contended that, in the case then under consideration, that limit had been overstepped. A clergyman might use his reason to ascertain the meaning of Scripture; but, having ascertained the meaning, he was bound by it. To describe the Scripture as an expression of devout reason, or the written voice of the congregation, was to reduce the Bible to the level of other religious books which had been written by Churchmen of influence from time to time. A plain common-sense statement of the question, in its legal bearings; amply sufficient for all practical purposes, and to which it need only be added, that the rule it lays down must be regarded as applicable beyond the ranks of the Body for whom it was framed, and binding upon all alike, whether clergy, or laymen; upon all, without exception, who receive the Scriptures.

That Advocate took the course which was professionally proper, not only in confining his remarks to the limits within which clergymen might express their opinions upon theological subjects, but

Inspiration is Supernatural.

also in not going beyond those broad and general terms in speaking of Inspiration itself. Such an account, however, is for the close investigator insufficient. True, the Bible is 'sui generis;' it stands alone; but the point to be determined is, in what its peculiarity consists; what are its distinguishing marks as a *Record*. It is the "[1] Word of God, and not of men;" this fundamental principle we assume the inquirer to 'embrace, and ever hold fast:' the point on which he desires to be resolved is this; Through what channels, and under what conditions, precisely, has this 'word,' this message from the "[2] Most High God," come to "us men?" It is admitted that this communication was made through the instrumentality of "holy men who spake as they were moved by the Holy Ghost." Now, since that which they "spake" was for the perpetual use of the Church, we may,

---

[1] 1 Thess. ii. 13. [2] Acts xvi. 17.

we must infer that when those chosen instruments of the Spirit proceeded to commit to writing what had been revealed to them, they wrote under the same Divine guidance. With the Books, then, which make up the Bible spread open before him, and sending his thoughts back to the occasions when the several writers "took in hand to set forth in order a declaration of those things which" "God had revealed unto them by His Spirit," the candid inquirer would assure himself as to the 'nature' and 'extent' of the inspiration under which each wrote. The substance of the revelation is placed beyond the limits of such an investigation as we are supposing.

In what did the inspiration attributed to the Scriptures consist? and, How far did it reach? are questions to which the most reverential student of theology may be imagined as bending his anxious attention. Now, if it is reasonable to expect that

Inspiration is Supernatural.

GOD would impart some knowledge to the human mind by other than human means, then the necessity of inspiration is proved. For, properly, Inspiration is not the truth miraculously communicated to the mind, but the qualification for fulfilling the duty imposed upon the receiver of it; which was, to speak, or to write down, the truth imparted; or to do both. Now, the soul of man is so constructed by "GOD who gave it," that it sends its thoughts back to the past, to know its own origin; and onwards to the future, to become acquainted with its destiny: and unless these inquiries be satisfied, it is miserable. But on these subjects it has no innate knowledge; so that, unless it was the Divine purpose to send information upon them to man, he would be in the condition of one created with great powers, but destitute of the means of exercising them. With a capacity for understanding the past, and contemplating the future, upon the one and the other he would be wholly in the dark. 'I find myself' (he would say) 'to belong to a race concerning whose beginnings I would fain be informed, but information I have none. I have a consciousness of my immortality, of which I cannot be denuded; but respecting the futurity which awaits me, I am utterly devoid of light.' Thus restless would the spirit of man be, were it not the purpose of GOD to send him that information for which "his soul hath appetite:" so that we may justly conclude, that unless GOD would leave the highest of His creatures in a worse condition than that in which He has placed the lowest, on which He has bestowed instinct to guide them, He would impart to him the knowledge which he craves.

Now, in no other way is it conceivable that this end should be accomplished, but through the instrumentality of men brought beneath the influence of a Divine energy, first, *disclosing to them truths which they could not otherwise have known,* and then, enabling them to record what had been so disclosed. Of these effects the former would be 'revelation,' the latter 'inspiration;' a distinction which (though we believe it to be just, and indeed necessary to be kept in view by those who would possess clear ideas upon the subject,) is not essential to the main argument, the basis of which is a truth which has been uniformly believed by the Jewish and Christian Churches, from the very beginning to the present day, that thoughts unattainable by the ordinary processes of " reason, experience, observation, and association of ideas, or relative suggestion," thoughts respecting the past, present, and future, were impressed upon the minds of certain men whom GOD raised up, first, to receive those impressions, and then to tell them with the living voice to the men of their own generation, and to commit them to writing, "that their posterity," to the end of time, "might know" those truths, "and the children which were yet unborn."

And thus we are conducted to that which is the central idea, the essential point, in this whole question, *the doctrine of the 'Supernatural.'* Here there can be no concession; there must be no ambiguity. The Church is called to different forms of trial and of duty, at different stages of her history. At this moment, the service to which she is summoned, and in which her fidelity is to be tested, is to [1] defend THE SUPERNATURAL. 'Standing upon her watch, and setting

---

[1] "Christianity offers occasion for this opposition" [of the human spirit against authority] "by its inherent claims, independently of accidental causes; for it asserts authority over religious belief, in virtue of being a supernatural communication from God."—Rev. A. S. FARRAR's *Bampton Lectures,* "A Critical History of Free-Thought in reference to the Christian Religion," i. pp. 1, 2.

herself upon the tower,' she has, at a preceding period, seen the same enemy she is now called upon to repel, making his advance against the walls.

In the eighteenth century, the German Rationalists and the English Deists combined to resist the doctrine which had been maintained in all ages by the Catholic Church, that, in and through the Books of the 'Bible,' as we have it, "God has spoken." The (¹misnamed) Rationalists do not deny that a revelation has been granted, and that the Scriptures "*contain*" it, designing, in the use of this

---

[1] *Private opinion* is the fit name for this system; for it has no principles whatever, and refers to no standard. It is one form of the "struggle of the human spirit to free itself from the authority of the Christian faith, the less violent of the two" shapes in which unbelief has manifested itself. "In the first great struggle of the human mind against the Christian religion, the action of reason in criticising its claims assumed two forms, Gnosticism, or Rationalism, within the Church; and Unbelief without."

word, to establish a distinction between the Word of God as contained in, and as 'co-extensive with,' Scripture; in other words, to make out that not all that is found in the Books which, collectively, are known as 'Scripture,' is God's Word, but some parts only; a distinction unwarranted by Church standards, or Writers, and, in itself, futile. "A merchant showing a ship of his own, may say, All my substance is [contained] in this ship; and yet never intend to deny that his ship is part of his substance, nor yet to say that his ship is in itself." Such was the clever answer of Chillingworth when pressed with a like objection by the Romanists: as an illustration, it entirely refutes this 'fundamental theory' of the Rationalists.

It is not a little remarkable how, from different stand-points, and with very different aims, the Romish and Rationalistic Schools meet in an agreement to drag

Rationalism, its Demands.   165

down the pretenfions of Scripture; the one, to fet up Tradition, the other, Reafon. But, ftrange to fay, they do not permit thefe books to be accepted and explained as other books are; but they frame their own ftandard of what might have been expected. Conftituting themfelves the judges of what is "good and profitable unto men," they bring in a new fenfe which they term the 'verifying faculty,' a tefting power of an utterly irrefponfible character, which is to qualify them 'to refufe the evil and to choofe the good,' of the Biblical materials before them. Admitting what they find in the Old and New Teftament to conftitute a revelation, in fome fenfe, and taken as a whole, they eliminate certain portions which this inward fecret meafure of what is fit rejects. By a fquare thus arbitrarily framed, they try the contents of the feveral Books of the Bible; and their reafon is to determine how far the teaching found in them, whether it relate to the nature of GOD, or the profpects of man, is true or falfe. They feem to pervert and parody the rule, "¹To the law and to the teftimony," and to fay, 'To the human intellect, and to the bar of reafon,' "if they fpeak not according to *this* word, it is becaufe there is no light in them." You muft fufpend your verdict, (fay they,) until you have fifted the contents of the book which folicits your approval. Your fubmiffion is not to be yielded upon the profeffion, by this Volume, of any 'à priori' claims. In a word, their motto is, 'No affent, no infpiration.' At this door, were it opened wide, would come in all the fchemes, fpeculations, and fancies, and even herefies, that have ever propofed themfelves in the ftead of the "faith once delivered unto the faints." In this form of "philofophy," if in any, is to be

---

[1] Ifaiah viii. 20.

Rationalism, its Demands.

recognized the portrait of the "thief and the robber, which cometh not but for to steal, and to kill, and to destroy;" and if, eluding the vigilance of those who should keep the gate of the city of God, he should gain an entrance, it may be expected that he will proceed to the citadel, and there make havoc of all that is distinctive and essential, in the Religion of the Bible.

Now, it were possible to go beyond these rationalistic-folk, and yet to come short of a right belief in Scriptural inspiration. 'But, stop,' (I can imagine some one here interrupting, and saying,) 'where do you find the canon of right belief,' on which you are so confidently pronouncing? If the belief is 'right,' then there is no more controversy. Is it a private dogma which you are about to enunciate? or, if not, what is its authority? A most reasonable inquiry; and, in its consequences, very important: for, if the reply shall be incontrovertible, then the question, 'What is inspiration?' may be regarded as finally answered.

The measure, then, of 'right belief,' which we are to hold in our hand, to try any theory upon this subject, is *that which the Scripture writers have framed.* On what account did they themselves receive and obey the sacred books? was it because all the contents of them were good, and holy, and true? they believed this sincerely; but this was not the proper ground on which they went. They bore witness to this point, that the whole and every part of the Scripture [1] was given by Divine inspiration. The Church in all ages has maintained this. By 'the Church' (and here we are committing ourselves to something like a definition; of which, however, we have 'counted the cost'), we mean

---

[1] "The subject of the Revelation is received as true because Divine; not merely regarded as Divine because perceived to be true."—FARRAR's *Bampton Lectures*, 1.

those who wrote the Scripture, and those who believed in CHRIST through 'their word;' a description which will satisfy all, being that which the LORD JESUS CHRIST gives of His Church. We know that this witness is true. " With these," (says Owen,) "¹ I had rather venture my faith and eternal condition, than with any society, *any real* or pretended Church whatever." To the profession contained in these last words, he who now quotes them cordially subscribes, even as he agrees with that Writer, that the Church (so interpreted,) was most uncompromising in the point referred to. With this precedent before our eyes, it were unlawful to fall down to any inferior standard. To receive the Scriptures upon any other, any lower ground, is, as the same writer has said, " to compound the matter with the world:" a remarkable expression, suggest-

---

[1] "The Reason of Faith."—Works of JOHN OWEN, D.D. Lond. 1823. Vol. iii. p. 266.

ing the thought that the attempt to try the contents of the Bible at the bar of human reason before giving in an adhesion to them, is essentially "of the world," the growth of man's pride and presumption. The world says, 'I am ready to allow, and to make use of this book, provided that the grounds upon which I accept it, have been settled; if it be distinctly understood on what footing I receive it, which is just this, that having read it throughout, I have come to the conclusion that it teaches nothing but what is found to be 'good and profitable unto men.' In a word, 'The Board' of Reason, having 'sat' upon the claims of the Scripture, gives its 'Testamur,' 'Examined and Approved:' the candidate has passed, is even classed ('in Literis humanioribus'), and has a 'Degree' conferred upon it. But the Church, which, in this, and in all things, is to be our guide; the Church as composed of the

Self-evidencing Light. 171

first writers of Scripture, and the feed of true believers, gave [1] no countenance to this method. They have not left us an example of *patronizing* GOD's eternal truth. "[2] Because our testimony among you was believed:" did the Apostle of CHRIST only mean that they had regarded him as a wise and good man, and so had listened to his communications? Do we imagine him, at the end of the Epistle to the Romans, with its logical dissertation on 'Righteousness by Faith;' or, the First to the Corinthians, with its 'great argument' for the 'resurrection of the body;' do we think of him as asking for the approbation of the individuals who composed the Churches addressed, and saying,

---

[1] "Non enim ideo inspiratum aliquid divinitus est, quia postea sit approbatum, sed ideo est approbatum quia fuerat divinitus inspiratum."

"*Censuræ Facultatum Sacræ Theologiæ Lovanienfis,*" A.D. 1586.

[2] 2 Thess. i. 10.

as the Roman actor to the audience, at the conclusion of the drama, "*Vos plaudite?*" So far from this, "he and Silvanus and Timotheus, for [1] *this cause* thanked GOD without ceasing, because when the Church of the Thessalonians received the Word of GOD which they heard of them, they *accepted* it as (admitted it as being) not the word of men, but, as it is in truth, the Word of GOD." Nothing short of this rises up to the full sense of the "witness" which the Church of true believers in all ages has given to the Scriptures. Wherein lay the essential guilt of those who in the time of the Prophets, denied the inspiration, and spake of their teaching as "[2] wind," and said 'The word is not in them?' Was it not that in such rejection of '*His* words in their mouth' they had virtually "belied the LORD," and said, in effect, "[3] Not he." To demur

---

[1] 1 Thess. ii. 13. [2] Jeremiah v. 13.
[3] Jeremiah v. 12.

upon the admission of St. John's Epistle as of immediate Divine authority, is to "[1]make God a liar;" for it is to disbelieve the "record that God gave of His Son," as through the word of others, so by the pen of "His servant John," at that very moment when he was writing his letter. These two instances deserve the most earnest attention, for they exhibit the refusal to acknowledge 'the word spoken by Apostles and Prophets,' as affixing upon the recusants the very high impiety of 'making God a liar;' the rejection of His Word given by His servants, being in each case so characterized.

It is a truth which, perhaps, is not vividly present to the minds of some who are occupied with this subject, that the Scriptures are to us, as the Apostles were to those to whom they preached in their travels, and living ministry. Not only do they supply the place of that personal

---
[1] 1 John, v. 10.

work; not only are they intended to accomplish the same end, that of bringing men to 'believe on CHRIST JESUS,' but they stand upon the very same ground, and present themselves with the very same authority. Let us in imagination place ourselves on "¹Mars' Hill," there with the "men of Athens," hearing Paul (who had "²seen JESUS CHRIST our LORD,") call upon the people who stood before him "to repent:" then let us try to realize the voice of the same Paul now, speaking to us the very words he used at Athens, as we have them recorded in the Book of the 'Acts,' and saying, Receive this "not as the word of man, but as it is in truth, the Word of GOD." Whatever argument he and Peter can be supposed to have employed wherefore their living teaching should be received by "all men everywhere," applies to us with equal

---

¹ Acts xvii. 22.   ² 1 Cor. ix. 1.

cogency that we should receive the Holy Scriptures. For, it is the 'record' itself that comes to us with the HOLY SPIRIT's seal upon it; and "GOD-breathed" is the inscription graven on it. Such, indeed, is the doctrine it contains, (for which alone the 'writing' is of any value): such were the men who penned it; and, pre-eminent among them, Paul, the author of this memorable compound '¹Theopneustos,' (a word ²peculiar to the Revelation,) the chosen term of the SPIRIT to whom it refers: but such, too, is the document itself, 'the Scripture.' Were men now to stand up in our congregations, or preach in our streets, bringing with them credentials of being 'inspired,' in the high and proper sense of that word, that is, of being immediately taught of GOD, we should listen to them with the most profound attention.

---

[1] 2 Tim. iii. 16.

[2] See TOWNSEND's "Scriptural Communion with GOD." Part i. p. 32.

Precisely such is the standing of the Scriptures in the midst of the Church. They are not one degree removed from the writers of them, in their divinity. "Moved by the HOLY GHOST were Paul and Peter, when at Athens, or at Jerusalem, they spake unto the people. Impressed "[1] by the same SPIRIT," and of co-ordinate authority, are the record of their living sermons, and the Letters which they wrote to the Churches.

We claim, then, for the inspiration of the Scriptures, the testimony of the Church; but we mean the Church of "all believers," ("Thanks be unto GOD for" that thoroughly Scriptural phrase, and for the inheritance of that venerable hymn in which it is enshrined); "the Holy Church throughout all the world," composed of "[2]all who in every place call upon the Name of JESUS CHRIST our

---

[1] 1 Cor. xii. 4.   [2] 1 Cor. i. 2.

Lord;" who have been "sanctified in Christ Jesus," and are therefore 'holy.'

Of the evidence that the Bible is the Word of God, which itself supplies, this is a part; but it is not the whole. "[1] If we receive the witness of" even inspired "men, the witness of God is greater;" a greater assurance to the soul. Let any call it enthusiasm if they please, it must be firmly maintained that the true foundation on which our acceptance of Scripture as God's Word must rest, is *the discovery of its inspiration made to and by the soul of each individual believer*, and that any other way than this is not God's way. He has spoken to the soul of man immediately by His Spirit in the Word, though He has employed a Prophet, or an Apostle, to be His amanuensis; and, by the soul to which He thus directly speaks, it is His purpose to be heard and

---

[1] 1 John v. 9.

recognized. And thus another important question will have been settled. The 'authority' of the Scripture, its binding claim upon our submission, depends upon its *perceived* inspiration. Marvellously exaggerated has been the weight attaching to the Church's attestation. External testimony, the suffrages of early Councils and Synods, is not without its value; nay, rather is it of great moment, within just limits: but the proper 'authority' is that which arises out of the Scriptures themselves to each student of them. When an inspired writer (and we know that such 'witness is true') says, concerning a great proposition, that it is ' [1]entitled to belief, and claims to be received by all,' he lays the stress of his assertion upon the doctrine itself. But, to receive any thing from a 'Church' as a Church, and to repose on this as our mainstay, is

---

[1] 1 Tim. i. 15.

to build upon a totally different bafis. 'Authority' over the human confcience no propofition or fet of propofitions can poffibly poffefs, except fo far as they are true, come they from what quarter of the Univerfe they may. The Scripture, "GOD's Word written," is true, becaufe it has truth in itfelf. The meafure of its truth is the meafure of its authority. Now, it is abfolutely true, becaufe it "proceeded and came forth from GOD." It is, therefore, abfolutely authoritative. Scripture 'fits a queen,' over all human minds and confciences fupreme. It can make no lefs a claim, being effential Truth, emanating from GOD Himfelf. Nothing more is required to prove that it needs not to be backed by any teftimony from without. The confent of the Church in its earlieft days, and in every fubfequent age, is rather the tribute paid to the majefty of truth, than the addition by as much as a fingle grain to the certainty of Scripture: "[1] I receive not honour from men."

The written Word of GOD takes up this ground as truly as did the Incarnate Word. [2] The Bible shines by its own light. An illustration (it is sometimes and truly urged,) is not an argument: some illustrations, however, are so striking that they are as satisfactory as logical arguments. Now, it has been remarked, that when the sun shines, no demonstration is needed of the fact: the glorious brightness of the luminary is its own witness. To produce evidence that the sun is shining, were not only superfluous, but the wildest folly.

Alike true, naturally and morally, is the 'dictum,' ' whatsoever *makes itself*

---

[1] John v. 41.

[2] See a Work by Dr. T. Jackson, (Dean of Peterborough, in the early part of the Seventeenth century): "The eternal truth of Scripture, and Christian belief thereon wholly depending, *manifested by its own light.*"—London, 1673.

manifest is light.' As true (though not the strict logical converse,) is the proposition, 'whatever is light, properly and essentially, makes *itself* manifest.' [1] "God is light:" His truth has its rise in the depths of His own Being; and he poured forth the rays of His essential light into the 'reasonable soul' of prophets, and evangelists, and apostles, when He revealed to them His truth. It was His light, and not their own brilliant genius, which 'shone before men' when they spake or wrote. Issuing from that spring, and introduced into the mind of each 'holy man of God,' the light was not diminished or dimmed, or in any way affected, by passing through the human channel, but came forth from the lips, or the pen of each, as pure and perfect as it first came forth from God.

[2] "Bright effluence of bright essence, increate;"

---

[1] 1 John i. 5.
[2] Milton's *Paradise Lost*, Book III. 5.

this, the poet's defcription of the Perfonal, is fcarcely lefs true of the written Word; "the moſt eminent reflection of uncreated light and excellencies."

This, then, is our conclufion. A Record thus 'born of GOD,' thus felf-evidencing, has within itfelf a witnefs to its own infallible infpiration, which extinguiſhes every other, even as the fun's beams vanquiſh the light of a candle found in the room which they enter; fo that it has been well faid that it matters not how the Scripture has come to us, whether by a child or a church; by accident, (were there fuch a caufe,) or by tradition; by confent of men voting it to be Scripture, or by Providence; to us it has come, with convincing evidence contained within itfelf, that "[1] GOD is in" it "of a truth." To the fpecial providence of GOD, no doubt, we owe it that the

---

[1] 1 Cor. xiv. 25.

Sacred Books have thus come to us, hiſtory proving that in this and other lands, the ſpirit of perſecution was hot againſt the authors, and would fain have cruſhed both them and their Works.

And, like as we owe no obligation to the Church of the paſt, ſo, beſides that of being [1] "a witneſs and keeper," a truſtee, we aſſign no importance to the Church of the preſent day, as though it *upheld* Scripture. When, in a Chriſtian ſociety, "[2] the pure Word of GOD is preached, and the Sacraments duly miniſtered according to Chriſt's ordinance;" when its "[3] children" are "found walking in truth," ſuch a church is "[4] holding forth the word of life," exhibiting and

---

[1] Twentieth "Article of Religion;" "Of the Authority of the Church."

[2] Nineteenth "Article of Religion;" "Of the Authority of the Church."

[3] 2 John, 4.

[4] Philipp. ii. 16.

recommending, but not sanctioning, the truth of GOD. Its tendency to produce such results, with the experience of them in fact, is the legitimate, the real testimony to the divinity of Scripture: any other is either artificial, or altogether subordinate. When minds are enlightened, and consciences awakened, and 'unruly wills ordered,' by the ministration of GOD's Word, he who feels or sees such effects is thereby led personally, intelligently, unalterably, to "set to his seal that" Scripture, in its every part, is "GOD-breathed."

The Florentine poet has a singularly apposite passage, where St. Peter, questioning him concerning his faith, asks:

[1] "And how didst thou obtain
The gem so costly whereon rests the ground
Of all the virtues?"   "That unstinted rain,"

---

[1] "Questa cara gioia,
Sovra la quale ogni virtu si fonda,
Onde ti venne?   Ed io: La larga ploia

Church-testimony exaggerated.

> I answered, "Of God's Spirit, which is poured
>   O'er the New page and Ancient, doth so plain
> A syllogism, to prove me this, afford,
>   That every demonstration, to be told
> Thereafter, would appear an edgeless sword."

See how, more than five centuries and a half ago, a mind of the highest order confesses that the grace of the HOLY SPIRIT poured out upon the Writings of the Old and New Testament, had wrought so pointed a conviction of their truth, that, in comparison, all formal demonstration seemed weak.

A general representative Assembly of all the Churches in Christendom, (were such a convention possible), which should add its own subscription and seal, as a

---

> Dello Spirito santo, ch'e diffusa
> In su le vecchie e in su le nuove cuioia
> È sillogismo, che la mi ha conchiusa
> Acutamente, sì che in verso d'ella
> Ogni dimonstrazion mi pare ottusa."

—DANTE: *Del Paradiso*, cant. 24to. 89—96. Translation, by C. B. CAYLEY, B.A., London, 1854.

Catholic Body, to thofe of all the particular Churches that have ever met, or made 'Declarations,' from the Apoftles' day to the prefent hour, could not confer upon the Scriptures the leaft particle of authority: of this their intrinfic truth is the fole and fufficient bafis.

"[1] Mafter, we would fee a fign from Thee:" fuch is the demand of thofe, in every generation, whofe characteriftics are the fame as theirs who firft made it. But "there fhall no fign be given," other than that which the wifdom of GOD has appointed. The 'felf-evidencing light of the Scripture,' as it has been well termed, is the true ground of belief in its infpiration; 'true,' becaufe it is in this way that it has "feemed good in" GOD's "fight" to 'give' *moral* 'affurance unto all men,' that in thefe Scriptures He "[2] has fpoken." 'He that' is thus

---

[1] Matt. xii. 38, 39.   [2] Heb. i. 1, 2.

brought to 'believe on the Son of God, ¹ hath the witnefs in himfelf:' not, however, any private whifper this, or fecret difcovery made to the foul; nor a fpiritual operation unconnected with the ufe of means, but the teftimony of the Holy Ghost, patent to, and to be judged of by all, by a folid and enduring work in the principles and the life of him who fo believes.

It will be perceived that thefe views are not in agreement with, nay, are directly oppofed to fome which have been put forth upon the fubject. A valuable Work, which has recently appeared, has received only qualified praife from fome critics, on the ground that it "omits 'the teftimony of the Church' to the infpiration of Scripture, fuch outward teftimony" being "in point of fact, *the main bulwark* of the true doctrine of infpira-

---

[1] 1 John v. 10.

tion, to which other arguments appealing to the reason of the case are rather supplementary." When the author of these strictures goes on to state that the cause of Biblical-inspiration does not hang upon so precarious a thread as that of our own inferences, from what we may have discovered of a supernatural character in the facts recorded, but "rather" upon this, that "we are told, upon competent authority, that" the Scriptures "do come from GOD," we should gladly find his meaning in "the testimony of the Scriptures to themselves; or, in other words, the account given of the nature and channel of their message by men whose divine commission is already and independently established; the testimony, above all, both of the Apostles and of our Lord Himself, to the divine authority of the Old Testament, and so, by analogy, of the New also." But we are forbidden so to explain the language of the critique, because it explicitly asserts that outward testimony is *the* true support of the pretensions of Scriptural inspiration; a proposition which it has been the design of the preceding remarks to controvert.

External testimony (in which we include arguments of every kind not drawn from "what is read" in the Scriptures themselves), is analogous to tradition. Tradition is not an assessor with Scripture upon the throne of judgment, but sits in a lower place; and its voice is listened to, so long as it preserves its distance respectfully, speaks in a humble tone, and is content to suggest modestly what may be, without presuming to pronounce what is, the meaning of any sentence that is heard from the throne itself.

CHAPTER IX.

Inspiration and Human Genius essentially different.

THE view just expressed, that by the light which shines from the Scripture itself, we discover its inspiration; and the assertion of the Rationalist, that "the nature of inspiration can only be known by the examination of Scripture," at the first glance seem so much alike, that the author of the latter sentiment (to employ his own phrase), might be [1] "ready to shake hands with those who,"

---

[1] " Essay " vii. p. 344.

Scriptures, how falsely measured. 191

he thinks, "use the same language with himself." But more than "a doubt insinuates itself," whether that language of ours, in which he fancies that he sees agreement with himself, do really contain such agreement. We are sure it does not, and that the difference between us is wide. For it is one thing to assert that the Book is a witness to its own infallible inspiration; another, that from an examination of the Book upon our own principles, and with a 'verifying faculty' "in our right hand" as our "line and plummet," we are to be the judges what sort of inspiration is to be assigned to it.

The 'freehandler' of Scripture declines to begin by asking whether it has said anything about itself, and its own authority: this, he thinks, would be to prejudge the question: he claims the right of determining how much or how little it ought to say. The Church, commencing from a different point of view, and with an *a priori* admission of Scripture authority, searches for any statements on the subject of inspiration, and having found such, regards the question, so far at least as respects the fact, as determined. The religion recognises, and so authenticates inspiration; and the evidence shines from the Book itself: which latter truth so far describes the *nature* of inspiration as to indicate a feature, an important peculiarity of it; but it stops short of any such account of it as would reach to a definition, for that should contain the essence. Many attempts have been made at defining in this case, some of which have come nearer, some have been farther off from what would fully satisfy our idea of inspiration as the characteristic of the Bible. To one it suggests itself as the impression on the human mind, by a Divine power, of a thought, or thoughts, respecting the past, present, or future, which it never could have obtained in the usual or human manner, by the exercise of its own faculties, or from the information of others.

On a point of such delicacy and difficulty, in which Scripture gives no help, (for, while the fact is unquestionably declared, nothing is found about its conditions, after a rigid logical manner), it seems safer not to venture upon a definition at all, but to confine ourselves to that which will be, for all practical purposes, sufficient; to offer an indirect rather than a direct account of the subject; to describe rather than attempt to define it.

The grand fallacy (if it be no worse, and have not its origin in any moral causes in the souls of the Authors), is, that inspiration "differs merely in degree from human genius." According to this theory, Paul the Apostle differed from the members of either of the Churches to whom he wrote, by possessing *ordinary* endowments

194 *Inspiration of the Holy Scriptures.*

in a higher degree than they; he stood highest in the scale of common gifts. Now, this we hold to be a most serious [1] untruth. Without any special, any extraordinary assistance, Reason may make its greatest efforts, and Genius achieve its most splendid discoveries. Newton may excogitate his immortal "Principia," and Shakespeare his equally undying dramas. Between the productions of these wonderful minds, and inspiration, an infinite "gulf is fixed." We speak of inspiration-*proper*, not recognizing that employment of the word by which it is made to signify an exalted state of the creative faculty, such as produces poetry of the highest order, or, indeed, any other great result, whether of that which is strictly called 'genius,' or of the ratiocinative

---

[1] "St. Paul was inspired, no doubt; so was Shakespeare. He who says this, intending no quibble, declares that in his belief St. Paul was not inspired at all."—*Sermons by* Rev. J. W. Burgon.

powers. The blessing of Him from whom "cometh every good and perfect gift," upon the mental faculties in their ordinary, their normal condition, accomplishes all of which the human mind is capable. The subject, indeed, is the same, in the ordinary and extraordinary operations: in both cases it is the soul of man, the same piece of Divine workmanship which is wrought upon, though the mode and the effect are, in each case, essentially different.

CHAPTER X.

'Extent' of Inspiration as respects the space.

HE foregoing remarks have dealt with the question of the 'Nature' of inspiration, negatively. A broad distinction has been claimed between human abilities, even in their highest form and cultivation, and the extraordinary immediate communication from God of truth which could not otherwise have been known. By genius and study man may rise up to eminent achievements in the

Inspiration, how far did it reach? 197

one; only by special Divine interference can he accomplish the results of the other.

The observations have not been other than negative, because anything more would have anticipated that which now comes on. Any positive statements would have run up into the question which is next to be considered, which is, the 'Extent' of this supernatural influence: *how far did it reach?*

Of this inquiry there are two aspects; or, at least, there are two views of 'extent.' The one is, over what *space* did it extend? How much of what we find in the Books of the Bible, is to be held as inspired? The other is, Of this inspiration, what were the proper marks? In what did it consist?

The former of these aspects will here occupy us. And, following the plan as before, we may enquire whether the Scriptures themselves afford us any help.

Here it will be necessary to examine, somewhat particularly, their language in one remarkable place; the last two verses of the First chapter of the Second Epistle of St. Peter : " Knowing this first, that no prophecy of the Scripture is of any private interpretation. For the prophecy came not, in old time, by the will of man, but holy men of GOD spake as they were moved by the HOLY GHOST."

Apart from one or two other critical suggestions to be offered, not as we deem unimportant, but yet subordinate, the true sense of the word "prophecy," as found in the three concluding verses, is that on which we lay the main stress. For want of a just apprehension of its meaning, a most important argument for Biblical inspiration has suffered loss. The general view of its import is very contracted. "Prophecy" is explained as 'prediction,' and as that only, whereas,

Contracted notion of Prophecy. 199

a prophet, in the language of Scripture, is one who speaks *for* GOD; not in His name merely, as an ambassador speaks 'for' the sovereign who sends him; not in His behalf, as an advocate 'for' his client; not in His stead, as a Regent acts in the realm 'for' the heir to the throne, who is as yet a minor: but a prophet is one who speaks 'for' GOD, as HIS instrument.

Of the two elements which compose the word [1] 'prophetes,' the former unquestionably does, as its primary and proper sense, mean 'before:' but this meaning disappears, or is modified, when it is compounded with the other and second element. Critics have asserted that the first employment of this term was to denote the interpreter of the predictions uttered in the heathen temples, for which they adduce authorities. But then, those prophets

---

[1] προφήτης

were so called, not as the authors, but as the 'tellers-forth' to the people of the meaning of the oracles. And if the word 'prophet' was by the Greeks applied to poets who, having begun by invoking the Divine influence, were supposed to write under the influence for which they had prayed, yet it was as 'uttering forth' their heaven-breathed thoughts that they acquired the name. Prediction formed no part of the task, whether of the Delphic functionary, or of the Grecian poet. In the case of the latter, it might sometimes appear in the brief and dark hints of the dramatic chorus; but it was there an accident, not a characteristic.

'A Prophet,' in the large and comprehensive sense which the word bears in Scripture, was one *in* whom the Spirit of GOD had made a revelation of truth to be communicated by the lips, or the pen, of that man. It may have been either prediction, or a warning meſſage, or theſe blended together: or, it may have been an exact acquaintance with hiſtorical facts. THE SPIRIT, ſpeaking firſt 'in,' and then 'by' him to the people, conſtituted him a prophet. There was within him a conſciouſneſs of the ſpecial entrance of the SPIRIT into his ſoul, which was to him the warrant, and an impulſe irreſiſtibly urging him, whether to 'ſpeak to the people,' or to 'write the words in a book.' He 'could not but ſpeak the things which he had heard.'

Any reader of the Old Teſtament throughout, whoſe mind had not been pre-occupied with the uſual limited acceptation of the word, could not fail to underſtand it in that large ſenſe which we have now claimed for it. The "Prophet" of whom the old Records tell, is one who ſpake concerning not only "things to come," but things belonging to the paſt, or his own time. The essence of his official character was that GOD spake in and by him.[1]

There is an expression found in the Gospels, which simply and compactly declares the *nature* of inspiration, and is worth a volume of arguments. Keeping it in memory, and often turning to it, the " way-faring men, though fools, shall not err therein." To the book-learned, and the unlettered, it is alike sufficient. We refer to the oft-repeated formula, " That it might be fulfilled which was spoken *of*

---

[1] In this sense, writers nearly coeval with the Old Testament period understood and freely employed the term. Josephus does so unequivocally, in these words: " As to the time from the death of Moses until the reign of Artaxerxes, king of Persia, who reigned after Xerxes, *the prophets* who were after Moses wrote down what was done in their time, in thirteen books. . . . From Artaxerxes to our own time, our history has been written very particularly, but hath not been esteemed worthy of like faith with the former, because there hath not been an 'exact succession of *prophets*" (inspired men) " since that time."—*Contr. Apion.* i. 8.

the LORD *by* the Prophet." GOD speaks; 'of,' in our translation, being, as we more commonly say, 'by;' and pointing to the *basis*-element, to the Author: HE speaks 'by,' that is, 'through,' a man, the instrumental-element. Compare herewith the words of the LORD on sending Moses; "[1] I will be with thy mouth:" and, as closely similar, those of the Apostles, when, quoting the Psalm, they prayed; "[2] Thou art the GOD who hast made heaven and earth, Who *through the mouth* of Thy servant David hast said." Words very remarkable for their full and explicit ascription to GOD, as the immediate Inspirer of what had been spoken, through David, indeed, but only as the channel for conveying them to man. It would not be possible to exaggerate the importance of this oft-recurring phrase, so much does it teach; the reference to it at this

---

[1] Exod. iv. 12. [2] Acts iv. 24, 25.

place in the argument, having been made with a special view to the light it throws upon the largeness of the meaning of the word 'Prophet.' For, it is to be carefully noticed, that in many of the Books to which that word, as found in the New Testament, points, no prediction whatever is found; making it plain that the term 'prophet' could not in that sense have been applied to the writers of them, by the Evangelists.

The words of St. Peter, in his First Epistle, do undoubtedly refer to 'prediction:' "[1] The Prophets witnessed *beforehand* the sufferings which were (to come) upon CHRIST, and the consequent glories" of His resurrection and exaltation: but, they do not in any way militate against the interpretation claimed for "written prophecy;" a phrase, (as we hold,) identical with, '[2] The whole of the Old Tes-

---

[1] 1 Pet. i. 21.
[2] As confirmatory of this view, compare Luke

St. Peter's use of 'Prophecy.'

tament-Record,' without any diftinction of the fubject-matter of its feveral books.

None will fuppofe that when, in terms manifeftly taken from St. Peter's words, (in his Firft Epiftle,) the Nicene Creed fays that the HOLY GHOST "fpake by the Prophets," the affertion is to be underftood as limited to the properly-predictive portion of their writings.

The term which, as ufed by Peter, is thus fhown to have covered the entire *Old Teftament*, is by his "[1] beloved brother Paul," applied to the writers of the New.

Let this be well weighed, for we are now on fpecially important ground; fince, if it be made good, we fhall poffefs, from two Apoftles of Chrift, jointly, a teftimony to the infpiration of the whole Bible: of the whole Old Teftament, in explicit terms, by one; and of the New,

---

xxiv. 27. (the eye being kept on the original), with St. Peter's words, 1 Ep. i. 11.

[1] 2 Pet. iii. 15.

as implied, by the other. For, by a comparison of the fourth and fifth verses of the Third Chapter of the Epistle to the Ephesians, with the fifth and two following of the Sixteenth to the Romans, it will be seen that all the Apostles were 'prophets;' and that their Writings were 'prophetical writings;' the latter phrase answering exactly to that used by St. Peter, in which, it has been shown, he comprised the *whole* of the Old Testament.

Close inspection, here, will lead to the conclusion that 'Prophecy,' in its legitimate, its proper sense, is *The Total* of Scripture.

Great light will thus be seen breaking in upon the Passage in St. Peter already indicated; a portion of Scripture which has engaged the careful thought of many learned men, and of which, as bearing in so direct a manner upon the question of

St. Peter's use of 'Prophecy.'

Biblical Inspiration, it may be permitted us to present a paraphrase in its integrity, and so to take the surest course for a right understanding of the important argument it contains.

'Now, we have what is more assuring,' (as a testimony to CHRIST as the Son of GOD, which was the subject of that voice from heaven, but of which voice, though attested by myself and those who were with me, you might either be doubtful, or regard it as a precarious foundation whereon to rest your faith, in so important a matter,) 'the record of prophecy, which deserves your most earnest attention, as being a light shining in a dark place, (this world).' Omitting any paraphrase of the remainder of this verse, as not essential to the argument, the following may convey the sense of what remains of the chapter: 'Recognizing this as a first principle, that no prophecy of Scripture,' (that is, no part of the Old Testament Writings,) 'springs from any private resolution' (or discovery).

'For it was not by' (any) 'will of man that prophecy' (the Old Testament Scripture) 'in old time was introduced; but, borne forward by the HOLY GHOST,' (certain) 'men set apart by GOD (for that special purpose, '*inspired men*') spake,' (and wrote).

A few words of comment upon the Passage so paraphrased. In the outset of his statements we are told, by an Apostle of Christ, that he is about to enunciate a fundamental 'principle, to be submitted to without further dispute.' What he does say, then, is an inspired axiom. Now we know that upon a mathematical axiom, the weightiest superstructures are raised. Grant the first principle, and all is built up: everything then follows in easy order. Attempt, after that the edifice of reasoning has been raised, to withdraw that axiom from beneath, and the whole building falls. Carry this analogy to the particular Truth for the fake of which the Apoftle demands that it be owned; and you will fee the immenfe importance of the doctrine of Infpiration. St. Peter tells us that it is a foundation-principle; the 'beginning;' the ftarting-point of all right views upon any other matters.

Of this confefledly difficult paffage any adequate [1]criticifm would extend to an

---

[1] 1. πρῶτον is equivalent to ἀρχή. 2. γίνεται (not ἔστι, with which the various explanations of the Paffage all agree in confounding it), properly expreffes 'origination.' 3. ἰδίας ἐπιλύσεως is the principal difficulty; the ftrict rendering of which, perhaps, is '*private* (or, *uninfpired*) *refolution;*' the words referring to the original Author of the προφητεία, the 'Prophet' himfelf, not to the modern interpreter; although ufually, and almoft invariably, they are fo explained, to the perverfion of the fenfe as conclufively determined by the following member of the fentence. To 'fpeaking by the impulfe of the HOLY GHOST,' in the latter claufe, is oppofed,

inconvenient length. But, after all the suggestions which have been offered as to the meaning of the original words for "private interpretation," their sense would seem to be determined, beyond dispute, by the latter member of the sentence. What is the contradictory of the assertion that 'inspired men' 'spake as they were supernaturally moved?' Just this, that when any spake, it was as a 'private' man, in his 'individual' capacity. The Apostle, therefore, is here to be understood, not as forbidding "self-interpretation," (the explanation of any passage as if it 'stood alone,' instead of comparing it with other

---

'prophesying out of their own hearts:' (Ezek. xiii. 2). 4. Θελήματι ἀνθρώπου, (compare John i. 13) *human will* as contrasted with 'Divine communication.' 5. ἅγιοι, 'sacred' has, in the N. T., the peculiar sense of 'consecrated,' or 'set apart *by the special teaching and designation of the Holy Ghost*. Ct. Rom. i. 2, for this attribute as given to the writings of the 'Prophets' by name: and, v. 19, for 'Prophecy' as announcing the Gospel.

Paſſages;) nor as laying down any rule whatſoever, but as denying that any portion of the " Writings of the Prophets" '*had its origin* in private opinion,' in any views which the writers held, merely " as men."

This view of the meaning of the original of "private interpretation," (and which the Tranſlators may have deſigned to expreſs,) is ſupported by [1] Owen. " This, then," (ſays that writer,) " is the intention of the Apoſtle: The Prophecy which we have written, the Scripture, was not *an iſſue of* men's fancied enthuſiaſms; *not a product of* their own minds and conceptions; not an interpretation of the will of GOD by the underſtanding of man, that is, *of the Prophets themſelves*: neither their rational apprehenſions, inquiries, conceptions of fancy, or imaginations of their hearts, had any place in this buſineſs:

---

[1] Vol. iv. p. 397. Works. Lond. 1823.

no felf-afflation, no rational meditation, 'managed at liberty by the underftanding and wills of men,' had place herein."

Thus Scripture has, again, helped us in our inquiry. We faw before how it afferts the *fact* of its own infpiration: now we have heard it declare the compafs of ground which that affertion includes. A great point this to have reached. St. Peter's Second Epiftle thus ftands out before us invefted with peculiar intereft: for, befides its other important announcements refpecting the " Day of the LORD," and "The New Heavens and New Earth," it contains thefe two doctrines bearing directly upon the main fubject; that St. Paul's Epiftles are an integral portion of 'the Scriptures:' and, that *the whole* of the Old Teftament is infpired.

CHAPTER XI.

'Extent' of Inspiration, as respects its quality.

THE question concerning the 'extent' of Inspiration, in its other aspect, of *quality*, may, perhaps, be more simply expressed thus: In what *sense* do we understand the writers of the several Books of the Bible to have been inspired? What do we attribute to them? In attempting to furnish an answer to this the essential point in the whole inquiry, we are quite alive to the difficulty, and, it may be even said, the responsibility, which is involved. Equally sure are we that it is impossible for the most anxious thinker upon this, or any other subject, (those, especially, on which the minds of men have been excited by controversy), so cautiously to shape his words, that they shall defy misinterpretation.

Now, those who have dealt with this very difficult point (for it is, unquestionably, among the "deep things of GOD"), seem to range under two main divisions; those who contend for the *words*, and those who are satisfied to regard the *substance*, as having been inspired. Of these theories, it may be said, in passing, [1] that the former seems to be quite irreconcileable with the free exercise of their faculties by the writers; receives no support from Scripture; is not required by the conditions of the case; is inconsistent with the fact of the existence of various readings; and subverts the authority of translations for conveying the meaning of

---

[1] See "Divine Inspiration," by E. HENDERSON, D.D., Lect. viii.

Verbal Theory untenable.

the Scriptures, whereas Truth admits of being construed. To these considerations let the following be added, that the theory is, in fact, untrue. Different words are used to describe the same event; and, sometimes, in those words are involved small discrepancies in the matter referred to, or in their aspect and relations to the whole subject. Now it is inconceiveable that such diversity in the narrations should have existed, if the words employed by any one narrator of an event had been exactly dictated by the HOLY SPIRIT; for then, any departure from that precise formula would have been a departure from the mind of the SPIRIT presenting the event or the doctrine after the one manner which by the decision of that infallible SPIRIT would alone exhibit it in its truth. When these several considerations are added together, they form a cumulative argument against the 'verbal theory,' which it would seem impossible to resist.

But what neceffity is there for fyftematizing in the matter at all? In its ftructure, as it comes to us, the Bible is the moft unartificial of books. Why, then, fhould it be fubjected to rigorous laws of any kind, when we would account for the method in which it was originally framed by its Divine Author?

May we not be excufed from the obligation to fubfcribe to the Procruftean theory of verbalifm, or any other which has been offered, and deal with the cafe as it comes to us, upon fome fimple principle, either fuch as would fatisfy us in "earthly things," or fuch as muft content us when the fubject with which we deal belongs to " things " that are "heavenly?"

To put the matter then in the plaineft poffible form, we hold concerning Scriptural infpiration, what would feem to be the common fenfe view of the cafe, that the HOLY SPIRIT fo 'guided and governed' the minds of His fervants whom He raifed up to write the several books which make up the Bible, that what they jointly left upon record should convey all the truth which it was GOD's purpose to deposit with His church, and should be free from aught which could mislead the soul. If these points should be secured, the end of Divine Revelation would be accomplished. But it is to be constantly borne in mind, that it was His TRUTH which "the Most Mighty GOD" willed to communicate; something which existed before, and soared high above, and was to outlast, and, for all these reasons, was independent of, any forms of language whatever; and, if so, then of the words, and syllables, and letters, of which all language is composed. It was through the medium of language, indeed, that the communications of the 'Infinite' were to be made to the 'Finite,' the message of the Creator sent down to the Creature. But language itself is GOD's creature;

and He did not place Himself in bondage to it. He employed it, as He did all the other agencies He had created; but still only as an instrument; as a means to an end; that end being the impartation to His reasonable and responsible creature of the knowledge of His will. Now, this knowledge would be attained through certain dealings with men and nations, to be historically made known; but, upon a scale of such breadth, and with features so large, as to be independent of words regarded in their minuteness, and to be capable of being "known and read of all men."

Such a view of the *end* for which the Bible was given to man does not open the door for any uncertainty as to its contents. The alleged facts are real occurrences: they are not fictions out of which instructive lessons are drawn, as 'Morals' out of 'Fables:' the things which "are written for our admonition" did really befal the "fathers" of the Hebrew people; they are true hiſtorical events, which "came to paſs" in the life of the Iſraelites before they came to us as precedents ('types') of the way in which GOD would always act under the like circumſtances. But ſtill, amid the diverſity of the occaſions, and with a leſſon ſpecifically different taught by each, they were placed upon record with one general aim, "to the intent that we ſhould not luſt after evil things, as they alſo luſted." This was the warning inference to be deduced from all the caſes; while, in particular, idolatry, wantonneſs, abuſe of the longſuffering, and murmuring againſt the diſpenſations of GOD, were for ever rebuked by the conſequences they then entailed upon thoſe who were guilty of them. In the Narratives, however, of the particulars of the ſinful conduct ſo puniſhed, the words were of leſs moment than the facts; and, if the latter ſhould be told in a manner substantially true, the former would have done their office. To contend that every syllable and letter was prescribed to, and forced upon, the Pentateuchal-historian, by Divine Power, is to insist upon that from which the mind revolts as a violence done to the laws of mind, and is a demand calculated to wake up more inward scepticism, than it will produce honest belief. For, "doubt comes in at the window, "not only" when inquiry is denied at the door," but also, when extravagant theories are thrust in as the conditions of orthodoxy. Such a 'golden image' has, however, been set up in the verbal theory, by some writers, and obeisance to it demanded, in terms as [1] intolerant as those of the Babylonish monarch. 'Whoso falleth not down and worshippeth' the 'dictum' that "in committing the contents of the Bible to writing, the penmen had all the terms im-

---

[1] Dan. iii. 6.

mediately supplied to them by the HOLY SPIRIT," 'shall the same hour be cast into the' infamy of 'rejecting the doctrine of inspiration,' in spite of the most explicit avowal of a "belief in its plenary and infallible characters." Full credit is given to the Authors alluded to, of being "[1] very jealous for the LORD," no less so, possibly, than the Prophet who thought that 'he only was left' to maintain GOD's cause. But, these good men (though, as we must think, not strongminded reasoners) may not assume that because they firmly hold a doctrine, therefore the aspect which it presents to them is the exclusively right one. We hold that it is possible to [2] bow submissively to the authority of Scripture, without subscribing to the opinion that its every word, and

---

[1] 1 Kings xix. 10.

[2] "Nec vero, id enim diligenter intelligi volo, superstitione tollenda religio tollitur."—*Cic. De Divinat.* lib. ii. c. 72.

syllable, and letter, was prescribed to the penmen of it; possible to believe that the HOLY SPIRIT took possession of the faculties of Moses and Ezra, of Isaiah and Daniel, of Matthew and Paul, so as to make them the organs for conveying His eternal truth to the Church, without admitting that, at the same time, He introduced into their minds whole sentences in a form as complete and fixed as the types in the compositor's frame, to which the printed page is exactly to correspond. We hope that many may be regarded as honest and consistent believers, who would decline to assent to such a scheme.

"[1] All Scripture is GOD-breathed." This asserts that the writings to which collectively, we have, by long habit, given the name of 'Scripture,' and which, mentally, we may think of as though they were one Document, were penned, "or sanctioned, by men who were under the

---
[1] 2 Tim. iii. 16.

special and extraordinary influence of the HOLY SPIRIT;" and that "they are the result of the exertion of this influence." "[1] Every thing which was written aforetime was" (so) "written for the end of teaching us:" even a Passage in the Psalms, the evangelical application of which is to CHRIST, comes under this law; so deeply struck are the roots, so wide-spreading the branches, so diversified the fruits, of Inspiration. But, neither of the last-cited Passages, though forming jointly a strong bulwark of that doctrine, affirms, or can be shewn to imply, that the minute elements, (words, and the particulars which make up words), were sent to the tongue and hand, in the same manner as was the substance of the truth to be taught, to the thoughts, of those persons whom the SPIRIT employed.

In a review of Passages which are frequently claimed as supporting the theory

---

[1] Rom. xv. 4.

now being considered, we may by no means omit one of which it is maintained that it expressly asserts verbal inspiration. "¹ Which things also we speak, not in the words which man's wisdom teacheth, but which the HOLY GHOST teacheth." In this sentence, following very nearly upon those often misapplied words, "Eye hath not seen, nor ear heard,—but GOD hath revealed them unto us by His Spirit," St. Paul contrasts the *manner*, as he had just contrasted the matter, of what he taught, with the style employed by the sophists and rhetoricians of Greece. As the doctrines, so the method of propounding them, differed entirely, in the one case, and the other. The "wisdom of this world" was appropriately exhibited in corresponding 'forms of language;' but, "GOD's wisdom," which needed not, and refused such recommendation, was expressed in the 'style which the HOLY GHOST sug-

---
¹ 1 Cor. ii. 13.

gested' as most befitting His own superhuman communications.

"Comparing spiritual *things*" (substances of truth) "with Spiritual," they would learn the "mind of the SPIRIT," and express it in a manner that should truly represent His design. The stress was not laid upon the words and syllables of man's wisdom, but upon what lay beneath them as either frivolous, or false: and so, it is not upon the words and syllables composing the language of the SPIRIT, upon anything so minute and microscopic, that the weight of the Apostle's argument rests, but upon the main ideas, the broad truths, which the phrases, whatever they were in particular instances, should embody. And it may here be stated, without fear of disproof, that the term "words," in the Passage on which we have deemed it important thus to comment at length, does not properly signify single, separate 'words,' such as a vocabulary, or the dictionary of a language would furnish. The term 'logos' sets before the mind 'a reason,' 'a principle,' some 'complex form of thought,' the exponent of which will be found rather in a combination of words and phrases than in these singly taken.

Finally, in our endeavour to rescue the term found in this thirteenth verse, from the sense of the 'verbal theorists,' we see the strongest reason of all in the employment of it in an earlier place in the same chapter. The Apostle, in the fourth verse, asserts that his 'address and his preaching' had not been presented to the Corinthians 'under the persuasive forms of oratory' so much used and so greatly relied upon by the Greek rhetoricians, but were of a wholly different character.' Now, it is very clear that the 'persuasiveness' referred to consisted, not in the use of single words, or choice phrases merely, (though doubtless it included both), but in the whole artificial texture of their style, and in the impofing effect which eloquence fo elaborated would produce.

A fimilar mifconception feems to prevail refpecting Infpiration, as is generally found on the fubject of Grace. 'Grace' is not any fingle beftowment; it is not the inftillation into the foul of any one faculty: but GOD's *gift* emphatically fuch, as the "[1]fufficient" fupplement of man's "weaknefs;" the "power of CHRIST refting upon us," not in one form, but "*according to our feveral neceffities.*" So, and fimilarly, GOD infpired His fervants the Prophets and Apoftles, not by bringing them all into a condition of mind abfolutely one and the fame, (how could this be the cafe, when their circumftances and their tafks were fo various?), but by enabling them, each for his particular work. [2] "Here and there" (Bifhop Hinds obferves) " are

---

[1] 2 Cor. xii. 9.
[2] " Early Chriftianity," Part II., Ch. iv., Note 56.

marks of an inspiration which dictates to the very letter; but, ordinarily, it is only a Divine superintendence, preventing error or omission, and interposing only for that purpose. GOD has enabled man to record and to teach His Word, as He has enabled him to do His will, not by superseding the use of his natural faculties, but by aiding them." If there was an entirely new revelation, the DIVINE SPIRIT would impress the original powers of the minds to be employed in communicating it, without suspending them. If prophecies which the utterers understood but "in part," were to be recorded, the SPIRIT would restrain them from every thing that was wrong, and supply what was defective. If historical facts were to be narrated; or, words expressly spoken by GOD as a message or other announcement, to be communicated, memory would be quickened, and "every failure or fault of it, miraculously remedied."

Nor is it denied that on many of these occasions, (even when the case does not necessarily imply it),—the very words may have been provided: doubtless they were whenever it "so seemed good" to the HOLY GHOST, whose agents the writers were. But our position is, that ordinarily it would not be so, both because such minute dictation would interfere with the free play of the mind, and also because it would be unnecessary. When a great moral philosopher, or a master in natural science, has settled in his mind the fundamental principles of some system which he intends to put forth in a treatise, this first stage (we may suppose), is succeeded by the arrangement, in his thoughts, of the parts of the Work, according to the relations of the subject. The [1] *matter* having been, in this way, completely *foreseen*, the words *follow*; not

---

[1] "*Verbaque* provisam *rem* non invita *sequentur*."
HOR. *Ars Poetica*, v. 311.

independently, but in the same manner as in a military expedition, the route having been fixed, and the march commenced, by those in command, the subordinates follow, upon a road, marked out for them, indeed, yet not passively, but with the free action of their feet, and of their wills. They are 'guided and governed,' but not compelled.

Is there not some analogy to be seen between this doctrine of Inspiration, and that of 'Free-will?' [1] "We have no power to do good works without the grace of GOD by CHRIST preventing us that we may have a good will, and working with us, when we have that good will." Even so, to Inspiration are essential two conditions: the truth to be, by GOD's instruments, communicated to man; and, the ability to communicate it: the one, and the other, supernatural. But, as the "miraculous qualification for receiving a

---

[1] X. Art. of Religion.

revelation, or other extraordinary knowledge imparted by GOD," was created in harmony with the univerſal laws of mind, ſo the "qualifications for fulfilling the courſe of duty ariſing out of it," (that of placing it upon record), were conferred in a manner that did no violence to thoſe laws. The mind was not diſturbed, nor its ordinary workings interfered with, when GOD's New Truth entered and occupied it. Equally free was it left to ſelect the phraſes, and their component words, when that Truth was to be written down.

The remarks which have hitherto been made in connection with the *ſenſe* in which we ſpeak of Bible Inſpiration, have referred to the views entertained by ſome as they are found on the ſide of 'exceſs.'

But, opinions are held and publiſhed, which appear both *defective*, and very miſchievous. Of this claſs the moſt glaring are thoſe which would eliminate from the Bible itself whole sections of what lies there, and even entire Books, by the application of the private, intangible, irresponsible rule called the 'verifying faculty,' on which some observations have already been offered. The parts of Scripture which these persons would cast out are such as, in their judgment, lack authority, or are intrinsically unworthy to hold a place among the writings by which the Church is to be taught what "to believe and to do." The subject is very wide, and forbids more being here said on it than that we [1] "receive all the Books," as "of the New Testament," so, too, of the Old, [2] "as they are commonly received;" understanding by this latter expression, not '*because* they are generally accepted,' but 'in the number and form in which they have been generally, by all the Christian world, ad-

---

[1] VI. Art. of Religion.
[2] "Ut vulgo recepti sunt."—Lat.

Eclectic Theories. 233

mitted:' "and account them canonical," on the ground[1] already urged, that they are entitled to be the "[2]binding Rules of our faith and religion, in their *own nature*."

It is afked by others, 'May not THE LORD and His Apoſtles have ſometimes ſpoken, as it were, unofficially, ſo that their words, on thoſe occaſions, ſhould be regarded as uninſpired? Is there not a parallel,' ſay they, 'in the conſtitution of ſociety?' In the learned profeſſions, we expect that the Judge, when on the bench, ſhall order his words with preciſion, becauſe he is then avowedly dealing with Law. We look for the like from the Phyſician, when he is holding a conſultation with his medical brethren upon the caſe of a patient, or addreſſing a body of

---

[1] *Vide* p. 134.

[2] Biſhop Coſin's "Scholaſtic Hiſtory of the Canon," (laſt chapter); the italics, as given in the text, being that author's.

students in the theatre of an hospital; as also from a Minister of religion, when he is speaking either from the professor's chair, or the pulpit. But each of these, the judge, the physician, the clergyman, performs many actions in which he is not distinguished from the other members of society; those, in fact, of which everyday life is made up. The common talk, the hourly movements, of the first, are not judicial; nor of the second, medical; nor of the last, theological.

Is there not a proportion to this in the case of the Apostles, and their Inspiration?

The fact is admitted, but not the inference. If "there were many *signs*" (tokens of His miraculous power, perhaps, more especially), "which JESUS did," of which no record is left, how much more likely is it that there were many actions of his life which have not come down to us? "But these" which "are written" admit of no eclecticism. No deed, no word, of the

Eclectic Theories.

Lord Jesus, which is found in the narrative as we have it, is unminifterial. The Holy Ghost made the felection, when He 'governed' the judgment of Matthew, or of John, to make that felection from the actions and the fayings of Jesus, the refult of which is found in their records, and thofe of their fellow-evangelifts.

There is yet another fuggeftion offered by thofe who fpeculate upon the 'extent' to which Infpiration reaches. Like that juft confidered, it does not imply any irreverence, or awaken the fufpicion of a fecret defire to reduce God's Book within as narrow limits as poffible. Whatever may be thought of it, whether it may be confidered as a tenable opinion, or otherwife, it is quite confiftent with a belief in revelation, and a general acknowledgment of the Divine authority of the Scriptures. It is fuggefted that Infpiration is not to be regarded as extending over the whole field of the Bible, but as confined to those parts of it which *involve religious truth;* what is properly and strictly such, doctrines and principles.

The mention of this theory seems to give an opportunity of briefly adverting to the fact, that the several Views of Inspiration which have been recently put forth amongst ourselves, are not new: they have prevailed at former periods in the history of the Church, and found, then, as strong supporters ranged under each, as the same opinions do now.

It appears that the [1] "belief in 'full inspiration' was held from the earliest times, with a few exceptions, and, uninterruptedly, until the Twelfth Century." Subsequently, there discovered itself, in the Seventeenth Century, in the Writers of Germany and of France,—represented respectively by Calixtus and Amyrault,—

---

[1] See Rev A. S. FARRAR's *Bampton Lectures*, (viii.), Note 50.

a tendency towards that very View of Inspiration which is now before us, as one of the suggestions of our own day. It may incline us to the cultivation of a tolerant spirit, thus to learn that opinions from which our own judgment may, possibly, lead us to differ, have been held two centuries ago by Christians of other countries, whose attention was thoughtfully fixed upon the subjects which excite so strong an interest, at this very time, among ourselves. Towards error upon fundamental points, no examples taken from other centuries and churches may make us indulgent. "If the foundations be cast down," what shall it avail to prove that the undermining process began some hundreds of years ago? But on questions which are plainly 'open,' it is a wholesome discipline for ourselves, to repress the "spirit which dwelleth within us," which "lusteth to" subjugate all around us to our own conclusions.

That thefe words upon tolerance are not a covert plea for our own adhefion to the View in queftion, will yet be made clear.

There remains to be noticed the theory of thofe who maintain that there is *no line of demarcation* at all, between the Bible, and other books; that it differs from other Works that the world has ever feen, in degree only. This School contend that we muft not carry any notions of our own about Infpiration, to the interpretation of the Scriptures; but that our belief on this point muft be made up of the impreffions we derive from the ftudy of Scripture. They hold, too, that Infpiration is the " voice of the congregation," not the voice of GOD *to* the congregation, communicating HIS mind upon things which had been " kept fecret fince the world began," but which are [1] " now made manifeft, and by the Scrip-

---

[1] Rom. xvi. 25, 26.

tures of the prophets, according to the commandment of the everlasting GOD, made known to all nations for the obedience of faith." These opinions, which characterize the Rationalism of Germany, have re-appeared (by contact, probably,) in the theological literature of our own country; 're-appeared,' for they originally began in England, and crossed from us to the Continent. It will be seen that this theory is in effect a denial of Inspiration, if by that term is properly meant Truth whose original "seat is the bosom of GOD," and which has been miraculously brought to our world by the "only-begotten Son, who hath revealed Him." "Great" as is "the gulf" between this last speculation, and that named immediately before it, the difficulty which that (the second of the views referred to), presents, is of such a nature as is not lessened by the fact that it has been widely adopted by many eminent and excellent writers in the English Church. The method of regarding the doctrinal portion only of the Scriptures as properly, or necessarily, inspired, seems to have had its origin in a 'pressure from without,' on the part of the deistical writers, to which many seemed to have yielded; a short-sighted and unwise policy, as we of this day may be inclined to think, since the spirit of unbelief will never be satisfied, but rather will take courage from the concessions made to its demands, and never rest until it have cut away from the Church every inch of the ground whereon its faith stands. To save the great *Doctrines* of Revelation from overthrow, (it may be), the deistical writers of that period were thus met halfway; while the views which they were the occasion of introducing, have found favour with many of our own time, who are not only infinitely removed from any sympathy with their loose opinions, but are to be ranked among the honest adherents to the true Faith.

But here seems to be the grand difficulty. Who can say in what part 'doctrine' is not contained? Where is he to be found, however "mighty in the Scriptures," who would encounter the responsible task, beginning with the first Book of the Bible, and ending with the last, of making a selection of such parts as should be pronounced to teach or to involve 'doctrine,' with the implied decision that the remainder were undoctrinal? Who would venture to draw the line between Chapters, (or other larger Sections), or even Verses, that do and do not contain, and were or were not designed to convey, religious truth for the instruction of the Church, throughout its generations, for ever? Where is the member of the Christian Church, who would gird himself to such a task, even if all his fellows would agree to commit it to him? or, What assembly of representatives of all the churches in Christendom would enter upon such an undertaking? or, if rash enough to meet for such a purpose, would not, as the fulness of Holy Scripture opened before them, 'go out, one by one, being convicted, by their own conscience,' of the [1] presumptuousness of the project to which they had committed themselves? Who can say in what part of Scripture is not contained some Divinely-inserted truth, or where some celestial ore does not lie embedded?

Our thoughts are here led on to another theory [2] already touched on, but of a character far too important, in its bearing upon the question of the *extent* of Inspiration, not to be more particularly noticed. A distinction has been attempted to be set up between the Word of GOD "con-

---

[1] " Periculosæ plenum opus aleæ
Tractas; et incedis per ignes
Suppositos cineri doloso."
               HORAT. Od. ii. 1.

[2] Page 163.

tained in," and that word as "coextenfive with" Holy Scripture. An old fubtilty, refuted when firft propofed; but not, on that account, lefs acceptable to minds whofe turn it would ferve, if, after two hundred years, it could pafs undetected.

Of the propofition [1] "Holy Scripture containeth all things neceffary to falvation," the more logically correct form, or at leaft, that which more clearly exhibits the defign of the framers of it, is, 'All things neceffary to falvation are contained (comprifed) in Holy Scripture,' fo that we need not, we may not, travel beyond its borders for any neceffary truth. It has been afferted, of the formulary above recited, that it does not deny but that Holy Scripture " may and does contain many more things" than thofe neceffary to falvation. The affertion may be true. But, apart from that formulary, and

---

[1] Art. VI.

irrespectively of the limits prescribed by that or any other ecclesiastical standard, we may determine the meaning of the word 'contained,' by the rule of popular use. When we speak of the 'contents' of a vessel, or of a chest, what do we intend? Plainly, *all* that is within either.

The word in question is misused, if employed to signify that GOD's Word is *to be found* in different parts of the Bible, but that not every portion of it is GOD's Word; that the gold ore is there for those who know how to pick it out, but that all is not gold. Historical evidence of the clearest kind can be produced to shew that the "[1]'Word of GOD' is an "expression commensurate and convertible with" the Holy Scriptures.

---

[1] "Whatsoever is GOD's Word is Holy Scripture: whatsoever is Holy Scripture is GOD's Word. They are equivalent and convertible terms."—*Testimonies to the Inspiration of the H. S. by the Rev.* A. M^cCAUL, D.D. p. 20. (Lond. 1862.)

It follows that the word 'contains' is rightly uſed when by it is conveyed the belief that every part of the Bible, without any reſervation, is GOD's Word; that the Scriptures are entirely made up of that Word.

As firmly, however, as we reſiſt the attempt to revive the miſinterpretation of the word 'contained,' muſt we maintain the liberty of underſtanding that term otherwiſe than it is very commonly accepted and employed. The error referred to is that of making the *words themſelves to be ends*. Apparently this is done; in effect it is, unqueſtionably, by many whoſe veneration for GOD's Book we hold in greater eſteem than we do their judgment. The latter faculty in theſe perſons is at fault, in two points of view: they do not diſcriminate; and, they do not foreſee conſequences. They do not diſtinguiſh between *the* "*eſſence*" *of truth*, and the *form of words*, in which it is 'contained.'

Much of what has been already said upon the 'verbal-inspiration' theory will fit into this place; for, the persons contemplated are the same; the cases, nearly so: since it is for the sake of sentences which the 'words' are to build up that the verbalists are so jealous of the single terms. But is not this question reducible to something like certainty? What is it which prompts a man to construct a number of single words into a sentence? Is it the affection he has for the words themselves? any interest he feels in them as spoken breath, or as written characters? Is it not that the mind has been visited by an 'idea' which it seeks to express by symbols that shall represent that idea to the minds of others? The man would share his thoughts (many, and deep, it may be), with others; and this he can only do through symbols as the communicating medium. If this be the true account of the matter, then must we ever look beneath the containing shell for that which it holds within. The body is for the spirit: now words embody thought. [1] "How needful to remember that the 'Word' of God lies in the essential *spirit* of the book, and not in its conventional form." Nor are they alive to the consequences which may be expected from insisting upon it. "For" (as the writer just cited remarks), "that theory tends to alienate all thinking minds from religion itself . . . . it clogs the Bible with a suffocating weight, by burdening it with claims unthought of by itself, nay, contradicted by the facts which lie upon the surface of its pages." As the mind of man finds an exponent of itself in the words which either the lips speak, or the

---

[1] "A Plea for Holy Scripture as the Treasurehouse of all-saving Truth:" by THOMAS GRIFFITH, A.M. (*v.* p. 19). London: Macmillan and Co. 1864; in which the whole of this question is ably and concisely treated.

hand writes, but those words centre not in themselves, but in the *idea* which called for their service, only to impart itself to the minds of others, while the thought is not so tied to the words which offer themselves as that they could not by possibility have been clothed in other phrase; so by analogy must we hold that the Mind of God, having His purposes and will to communicate to man, brought this to pass through tongues and pens which He moved effectually, but to whose language (though regulated by Himself),—the sovereign Spirit was not so bound as that no other series of sentences, or combinations of words making up any one sentence, could have accomplished the end for which He employed those intelligent instruments.

The remarks which have been made in this and the former Chapter, have been intended to furnish an answer to the question, 'How far Inspiration extends.' But

'Extent' stated Explicitly.

it may be well not to leave the 'doctrine' to be merely *gathered* from what has been advanced, but to state it, so far as is possible, in explicit terms. We hold that Inspiration covers "the whole face of the ground" of Scripture; and that there is no book, nor any portion of any, of that Collection of Documents which we know as the "Holy Bible," of which it could be said, That part is to be excluded, or may be excepted, from the inspired Word of GOD. 'Embracing writings of very different kinds,' some containing facts of history, some supernatural revelations, and others whose characteristic title might differ from either of these, whatever be the subject-matter peculiar to the several books, we maintain that the entire Volume familiarly known to us as "The Bible" is properly and truly Divine; and that could each Book, as it lies there, find a tongue, it would say concerning itself, "[1] I proceeded forth, and came from GOD,

---

[1] John viii. 42.

neither came I of myself, but He sent me" to contribute, in my place and proportion, to that total of truth which it was His will to communicate to Men, to educate them for an immortal existence.

A few cautions have to be added.

Some writers discover great anxiety to "distinguish between the 'interpretation' and the 'application,' of Scripture." 'Application' *by whom?* Unquestionably we may not employ "the words of GOD" in any way not agreeable to the Mind of God; that is, to His design in causing the words to be written. But that 'use' of Scripture which we find in Scripture itself, namely, of passages in the "Old" by writers in the "New Testament," is not to be spoken of as illegitimate 'application;' as an ingenious accommodation of words to occasions foreign to those which first gave rise to them, and therefore destitute of authority. Such an account of the matter involves a denial of

Inspiration, and reduces the writers so employing the words to men of imaginative minds, who, by the help of a lively fancy, were struck by a resemblance in sound where there was none in sense, and hence persuaded themselves of a coincidence (groundless, as it seems to the 'critics'), between the ancient and the new occasion; a similarity in words, but no more.

It is readily admitted that "the indiscriminate use of Scripture" by those (non-Scriptural) writers who force its language into the service of their own arguments, has "a tendency to maintain erroneous conclusions of every kind." But the distinction is broad between this case, and that of the *Scripture*-writers, who make a new use of what first appeared in the Old Testament: and, unless we are prepared to yield the claims of Inspiration over a very wide portion of the field of Scripture, we must stand by them here. The employment by the Apostles and Evangelifts, of the language of the Pentateuch, the Pfalms, and the Prophets, in other and deeper fenfes than belonged to the words in their original places, is a feature in their writings fo prominent, and fo pervading the whole texture of them, as will not admit of being explained away. A believer in the Divine authority of the Bible will recognize its divinity as very remarkably fhining forth in this peculiarity. '[1]Great is the GOD' of the Bible feen to be, 'in this:' His Truth 'waxeth not old.'

We muft beware, too, of looking for the *teft* of Infpiration in the accordance of the Scriptures with the purer light which fhall be found in man as the world grows older. A notion of this fort (not very clearly expreffed, it is true), is cherifhed in the mind, and forms a part of the fyftem, of fome modern

---

[1] Μέγας ἐν τούτοις θεός, οὐδὲ γηράσκει.
SOPH. *Œd. Tyr.* 871.

writers, who speak of the discoveries of God which the Bible contains, as destined to receive a testimony from the improved and ever-improving condition of man's nature. Whence this exaltation of the human character is to come, does not appear; but manifestly not through the Bible as its source. The old-fashioned doctrine has been that *by means* of Scripture truth, as God's instrument, the human character is to be enlightened and elevated. But the method here referred to is altogether different. We have, then, to make our election between the two; the Scripture as *witnessed to* by a 'shining light' in the human soul, (how kindled, and how fed, we are not told), 'shining more and more unto' some visionary 'perfect day' in the history of the human species: and, the Scripture, in the hand of the HOLY SPIRIT, its Author, as that by which the pretensions of all other schemes for enlightening man's mind are to be tried; a method which makes the Divine Word to 'bear,' but not to 'receive' witnefs.

The mifts which, in the opinion of fome perfons, furround 'Infpiration,' will (they affure us), 'clear away if we admit the principle of progreffive revelation.' What is implied in this language concerning the Book which contains the 'revelation' as we have it, is quite clear. For, fince 'imperfection, and even error,' attach to what is 'progreffive,' the inference as refpects the Scriptures cannot be concealed. But [1] we decline to be 'helped over the difficulty' (if there be any), in this way. It were hopelefs to follow fceptical minds into theories of 'perfection' or 'truth:' and even if we could underftand their 'ideal' of each, we fhould probably decide that it never could be realized.

---

[1] "Non tali auxilio . . . . . .
Tempus eget."—VIRG. Æn. ii. 521, 2.

Nor has Inspiration any cause to tremble from *scientific* difficulties. Let it be granted that recent discoveries in geology, or ascertained facts of chemistry, may be only the pioneers and precursors of other and higher acquisitions in these sciences. Yet the Bible has nothing to fear from any developments of these branches of knowledge, since it contains no statement connected with them which has ever been disproved. The human element has never been permitted so to predominate as to be the cause of the introduction of what is false into the Sacred Record. "Man" has not been allowed to "have the upper hand" to such an extent as this: his natural faculties have been employed by his Maker, and (as we believe), without interfering with the liberty of his will; but ever in subserviency to 'truth,' both as regards the main end of GOD's Revelation, and the particulars which make it up. It is not merely from a sense of what some have termed 'Divine-decorum,' that we maintain that mistakes of fact cannot be imputed to Scripture Writers, but from a conviction that no error was committed by them. The Bible is free from *real* imperfection: and if ever the language of the writers, when in their narratives they touch on scientific topics, seems to be at variance with our fuller information on such matters, the natural and satisfactory solution of the difficulty is to be found in this truth, that, to them the true theory, in each case, was not yet known; and that they described what they saw, or otherwise knew, in free and popular language. "If so, there is no need of elaborate reconcilements of revelation and science," since they have not been "severed" by even a "temporary misunderstanding." We have not to wait for an enlargement of the idea of Nature to enlarge that of Revelation, as though the terms of the latter should have to be explained away in deference to the higher authority of the former; the misty conceptions of Bible-writers to give way to the brighter light of the better informed in our own day. If recent criticism have had a dream of "[1] obeisance" to be "made to" its "sheaf" by the sheaves of the Old Testament historians; or that "the sun, and the moon, and the eleven stars," the venerated Scripture Authorities who have told us of "interruptions in the order of the world" on some special occasions, will, hereafter, "see the providence of GOD in" the *un*disturbed "order of it;" in other words, if it is imagined by those who press upon us the obligation of inquiring into the truth of alleged facts on the strictest principles of investigation, that Revelation will have to confess itself mistaken in some matters which pious people have been accustomed to accept as literally true, before the overpowering

---

[1] Gen. xxxviii. 9.

light " of evidence or experiment," which may hereafter break in upon us, it may repress the confidence of such expectations to remember that ¹ Time can supply more materials for the service, not of those only who resist the idea that any of the facts of Scripture are Supernatural, but of those also, who think it consistent with the soundest philosophy to believe that the ' emergency of a revelation' might justify (even if to Omnipotence it cannot be thought to have ' compelled '), ' occasional' extraordinary interposition.

Faith is not opposed to Reason, nor Revelation to Science: but Reason, exercised within the limits of its just province, will support Faith; and Science expounded by masters, and not by sciolists, will confirm Revelation.

With respect to the substance of Scripture, Inspiration sets up no theory in

---

¹ Ἀμέραι δ' ἐπίλοιποι
Μάρτυρες σοφώτατοι.

PINDAR. *Olymp.* I.

opposition to undeniable facts of history or philosophy, while in claiming the whole field of the Bible, it merely asserts that the total of the Bible comes to us with GOD's seal appended to it, the continual office of the Church being to extract, as it may, by the promised light of the SPIRIT, the 'profit' of "[1] doctrine, reproof, correction, and instruction in righteousness."

When GOD had finished Creation, He "[2] saw everything that He had made; and behold, it was very good."

When He sealed His Son, at his baptism, to the work of Redemption, He proclaimed by "[3] a voice from Heaven," that 'in him He was well pleased.'

So it is to be believed, that when He looked upon the completed Record of the Old and New Covenants, He decided it to be, for the ends to which He had appointed it, "perfect and entire, wanting nothing."

---

[1] 2 Tim. iii. 16.   [2] Gen. i. 31.   [3] Matt. iii. 17.

CHAPTER XII.

Some Heads, of Admonition to one clafs; of Encouragement to another.

N the arguments which have been employed upon this fubject, the clafs of perfons which we have kept in view has been that of candid and reverential inquirers, rather than of profeffed opponents.

The remarks, however, which remain will be directed principally to the latter clafs. A few words will then follow for the fake of a very different defcription of character, who ought not to be forgotten.

If any man is refolved to fhut his eyes againft the Infpiration of the Scriptures, until he has mathematical demonftration of it, fhut they muft for ever remain. For, there are [1] fome fubjects which are, from their very nature, incapable of being fo proved. The evidence of them is entirely *moral;* made up of a variety of confiderations which tell with great force when taken together, but which, when regarded fingly, may not feem to be of any great moment. So far, there is truth in the affertion that it is only by examining Scripture that we can come to know the nature of Infpiration; that it is whatever it is found to be, when the Books them-

---

[1] πεπαιδευμένου γάρ ἐστιν ἐπὶ τοσοῦτον τἀκριβὲς ἐπιζητεῖν καθ' ἕκαστον γένος, ἐφ' ὅσον ἡ τοῦ πράγματος φύσις ἐπιδέχεται.—ARISTOT. *Eth. N.* I. 3, 4.

selves have been read through, and considered. With the 'animus' which underlies such a caution as this, as originally uttered, we are not here concerned. We accept the principle it contains, in the full confidence that it will lead out, not to a lower, but a higher estimate of Scriptural Inspiration. Do not predetermine the character of the Bible, is a rule which will exclude injurious prejudices as much as it will undue prepossessions. As no conditions for entering upon the inquiry can be more fair, so none are more promising as to the result. For, of the myriads who from the time when the Canon of Scripture was completed, to the present hour, having read the Bible throughout, have been thoroughly persuaded of its Inspiration, how many, do we suppose, began with any theory at all in their minds? The "prejudication" which opponents of Inspiration would 'resist' had no place in their thoughts.

The single Subject is 'Religion.' 263

They began it, perhaps, (indeed it could not be otherwise), under those feelings of inherited reverence with which, in every Christian, or at least, every Protestant country, the Scriptures are regarded. But they ended with what was much deeper. They felt, from the first, a strong interest in the Volume, arising out of its subject, so closely touching themselves and their eternal hopes. They were attracted towards it, above all other Books, from finding it wholly taken up with these topics; that while the Writings which composed it differ from each other in structure and style, they have one common feature; *they all relate to God, and man's soul.* "GOD in History" is a striking thought, and fact; His hand discernible in all the events that have befallen nations and individuals: but the Bible goes beyond this; its immediate and proper subject-matter to us is, GOD in His relation to men; GOD speaking to, or dealing with our race, directly: this is, from the beginning to the end of it, the characteristic feature of the Bible.

Now, this is one of the moral evidences of the Divine origin of the Scriptures which silently and secretly makes its way with the soul; and has, in fact, "wrought" thus "effectually" with the countless thousands who, from the time that the Sacred Writings were first collected, to the present hour, have 'meditated therein day and night.'

This stealthy conviction of the divinity of the Bible, arising out of its devotedness to the one interesting subject, has been strengthened by the perceived adaptation of its truths to their own feelings and wants. The cravings of their immortal nature have been satisfied. They have found themselves in communication with a Mind that knew their own minds; they discover that the "[1] Father of" their

---

[1] Heb. xii. 9.

Searching and Inexhaustible. 265

"spirits" has been speaking to them throughout. The words have so searched the inner chambers of their being, that they "believe and are sure" that they are the [1]voice of 'Him that made them,' that they have come forth from "the bosom of God." They could not but conclude that the lock and the key which they have found to fit its wards with such exactness, were the work of one and the same Artificer.

In this, too, does the candid mind discover a powerful evidence of the divinity of the Scriptures, that they are *inexhaustible*. "[2]Whosoever drinketh of" the springs of human philosophy, or human genius, shall not only "thirst again," but shall find that the springs themselves run dry; whereas the supplies which the Scriptures yield are incessant, and endless. The

---

[1] . . . "Nec vox hominem sonat" . . . .
                    Virg. Æn. i. 332.

[2] John iv. 13.

experience of those whose lifetime has been absorbed in the study of them will bear witness that when we so speak of the resources of the Bible, we use not the language of figure, but " of truth and soberness;" and that they are, literally, "[1] like a spring of water whose waters fail not."

To these instances of moral evidence which the Bible furnishes may be added that of *harmony found in diversity*. Shrewd intimations are given by some Writers, of being anything but satisfied by the fact that "[2] the Scripture obviously embraces writings of very different kinds; the book of Esther, for example, or the Song of Solomon, as well as the Gospel of St. John." But what if that which is thus represented as heterogeneous, be found to exhibit an " agreement of its parts in the most unsuspicious [3] manner?" Then we

---

[1] Is. lviii. 11.   [2] Essay vii. p. 347.
[3] " Dissertation on the Inspiration of the New

have found a point of strength instead of weakness, in the diversity of the contents of the Scriptures.

The Authors alluded to seem to espy a drawback to the high pretensions of the Bible in "the mixed good and evil of the characters of the Old Testament, which nevertheless does not exclude them from the favour of GOD." Here, too, if we mistake not, is a feature which tends to create assurance rather than misgiving. Had the characters described as enjoying the Divine approbation been other than what we find human nature at its best estate, to be, we might well have been visited with mistrust as to their reality:

Testament," by P. DODDRIDGE, D.D. The immediate application of these words by the Author is to the *New* 'Testament;' of which, however, he says just after, that it is "in delightful harmony with the Old;" so that his language may fairly be adduced as testifying to the harmony of the two Divisions of the Bible.

but we have prefented to us "¹men of like paffions with" ourfelves, though in the main "²perfect and upright, fearing God, and efchewing evil;" refpecting whom, it is to be borne in mind, that their cafes are often introduced, not merely to fet forth what they were in themfelves, but as the occafion of noting God's dealings with them, as types of His ways with the like characters, in their mixed form, as they fhould always be.

For the clafs of Objectors whence thefe 'criticifms' have fprung, compofed as it is of perfons of acute minds, it is probably unneceffary to add a caution which neverthelefs, for the fake of others, fhall here be inferted. We muft beware of fuppofing that all the actions 'recorded' in the Bible are fo faid to be infpired, as if they were *approved* by the Author of the Scriptures. Not all the doings of perfons in the Old Teftament which are narrated,

---

[1] Acts xiv. 15. [2] Job i. 1.

are thereby commended. The words and deeds of evil men are not therefore commended by the HOLY SPIRIT, becaufe they have been made Scripture by Him; nor are the weakneſſes of good men put forth as points of excellence. In their failings we are admoniſhed, not what to imitate, but what to avoid. The diſtinction which Logic furniſhes may here be of ſervice. We are not to look to the *matter* of any narrative (whether it relate to perſons, or actions, or facts), independently of its conditions, as approved, or diſapproved by GOD. The *form* is that with which alone we are concerned in the queſtion of Inſpiration. "As they are Scripture, theſe things are of GOD:" but beyond this, nothing is, neceſſarily, to be concluded reſpecting them.

It is the taſk left to the Church, (which it cannot transfer to any imaginary infallible Head, and for which it is enabled by the promiſed aid of the HOLY SPIRIT, as its peculiar endowment), to interpret the

Record aright. In this respect the Scriptures may be thought to have a symbolic representation in the "¹net that was cast into the sea, and gathered of every kind."

The Writers who deny the Inspiration of the Scriptures, or who so lower the idea of Inspiration as to make what they would admit to be scarcely worth contending for, should also be reminded that they achieve no triumph by a legal decision that the doctrine in question has not been asserted in the Formularies of the Church. If it can be shewn that any " particular or national Church " is without a 'dogma' upon the point, such omission will necessitate their course to the Judges in a Court of Law, where the " letter," rather than the " spirit," must be the recognized measure. But every candid person, every seeker after truth, must perceive that the question of the real views of the Church itself is not so determined. Its 'doctrine,'

---

[1] Matt. xiii. 47.

in a forensic sense, *is* undoubtedly settled, when a 'judgment' founded upon the consideration of what the Church has or has not said, 'ex cathedra,' has been pronounced: but its 'belief' is not thus defined.

The omission in the "Articles of Religion" is easily explained. On that subject there was no controversy, at the time they were drawn up. Whatever other forms of error springing from the "[1] foes" within the "household" required to be combated, whatever other rocks and shoals called for the uplifting of a beacon-light, this of the open or covert denial of Inspiration was not one. No occasion, therefore, having arisen for an *explicit* 'declaration' of the Church's view upon this subject, we possess none.

Yet who that simply desired to ascertain the *mind* of the Church of England upon the matter of Inspiration, could fail to arrive at it by studying its standard

---
[1] Matt. x. 36.

Authorities, and its Services? The former, for the reason already assigned, do not 'settle' the matter of Inspiration, to a litigant; to him, and for his purposes, they unquestionably leave it open : while to one who, without any end to gain, and solely for the satisfaction of his own mind, inquires what the Church does really and firmly hold respecting Inspiration, the fullest assurance will be furnished, if not by what is said, yet by what is assumed, in the language of the Formularies. We need not go beyond the title of the "Sixth Article," which speaks of "The Holy Scriptures." Was this phrase the invention of the Framers of the Articles? or, of the Church of the Middle Ages? or, even of the primitive Church? Is it ecclesiastical at all? and, not rather, Scriptural, in its source, and derived immediately from the well-known [1] words of

---

[1] 2 Tim. iii. 15.

St. Paul to Timothy, in which, introducing the term "Holy" as an attribute of the "Scriptures," he immediately expounds it as equivalent to 'God-breathed?' The compilers of that statement, therefore, drawing the Heading of the 'Article' from that Passage, must be understood as meaning to affix their seal to the Apostle's assertion of the Inspiration of the Scriptures. Unless, then, we are prepared to maintain that the Reformers were indebted for the phrase "The Holie Scriptures," to their own wit, and had no eye to the Passage which we have alleged, we must hold, that after a manner most easy and natural, yet quite conclusive as to its design, they set up in this Formulary (regard being had to the Title, and the affirmation contained within the Article itself, taken together), a *quasi*-doctrine of Inspiration. This conclusion will be assented to by any one who compares the Passage of St. Paul throughout, with the language of the 'Article;' the instruction which is '*effectual unto salvation*' being the point dwelt upon in both.

The reasons which have been offered as accounting for the absence of any express mention of Inspiration, in the dogmatic Statements of the Church now, apply in a general sense to the Jews, and the Primitive Church. There was never any doubt among either upon the point. Their notions may not have been very sharply defined; but there is abundant testimony to prove that they never admitted into the Canon any books which they did not believe to be the "Books of God." Rationalist Divines admit this; and, by such admission, prove all for which we contend, since if Inspiration was a *sine qua non* to obtain for any book a place in the 'Rule of faith,' its reality in the estimation of those who advanced it to such a rank, is as fully established, as if a 'Declaration' respecting it had been drawn up and subscribed.

If all these considerations be allowed their just weight, they will serve as a check to the confidence of those Writers who persuade themselves (if, indeed, they do really so think), that because a Church has not said formally, 'I believe that the Scriptures are inspired' (*eo nomine*), it therefore either does not so believe, or is to be understood as designedly leaving Inspiration an open question.

If it be true that there are "signs that the divisions of the Christian world are beginning to pass away," such a cheering prospect must rest not upon a supposed readiness to receive a more 'rational' method of dealing with the pretensions of Scripture, but upon a disposition in Christians to think less of mere sectional distinctions, and to unite in [1]'*earnestly contending* for the faith which was once delivered unto the saints' upon the old (but not 'antiquated') principle, that the Scrip-

---

[1] Jude 3.

tures are the depository of that 'faith.' The "restoration of belief" (if, indeed, it be decayed), is to be looked for, not by removing any imagined incrustation with which a weak acquiescence in the notion of supernatural Inspiration had overlaid it, but by a return to that state of mind which led the unsophisticated believers of the early days to open their eyes and their hearts to the evidences of the spoken and the written Word. For, those men are not to be thought of as unreasoning and credulous, but as no less competent than any of the shrewd people of our own generation to [1] "judge of the doctrine whether it" were "of God," or not. The [2] "multitudes both of men and women" who through the personal teaching of the Apostles "were" first "added to the LORD" as "believers," and "continued steadfastly in the doctrine" of "their teachers," and were [3] 'built up' into

---

[1] John vii. 17.   [2] Acts v. 14.   [3] Acts ix. 3.

enduring Churches by their Letters, began and persevered upon rational conviction.

The preaching of the Apostles was attended with a [1] 'powerful demonstration of the SPIRIT,' and their Letters were confessed to be [2] "weighty and powerful:" both were addressed to serious and honest-minded men, and the effect is told in the words, [3] "*Therefore* many of them believed." The restoration of belief may be expected to follow upon the restoration of Beroean candour. If this 'golden age' of faith is to come back, the sign of its return will be the simplicity of mind which marked the Christians who framed the Canon of Scripture. They found, in the Documents to which they were led to "set to" their "seal," holy matter treated in a heavenly manner. In the union of these two features they saw "a peculiar character distinguishing these writings

---

[1] 1 Cor. ii. 4. [2] 2 Cor. x. 10.
[3] Acts xvii. 12.

from all writings of a human original, and manifesting them to be of GOD."

Were we to shrink from professing our belief that saving faith in the hearts of individuals is the work of the HOLY SPIRIT sealing and witnessing to them the truths of the Scripture, we should show ourselves "ashamed of CHRIST." Not less untrue to our convictions should we be were we to hesitate to avow our belief that the Inspiration of the Scripture itself is to be known by discerning GOD's "work in His Word." His truth, just because it is His, and stands so related to Him, imparts to the *Word* of His truth an ineffable greatness and power, and "draws the soul to agreement ¹beyond" the power of any "systems of logic, or mathematical demonstrations." If so, then

---

¹ Πίστις ἡ ὑπὲρ τὰς λογικὰς μεθόδους τὴν ψυχὴν εἰς συγκατάθεσιν ἕλκουσα, πίστις οὐχ ἡ γεωμετρικαῖς ἀνάγκαις, ἀλλ' ἡ ταῖς τοῦ πνεύματος ἐνεργείαις ἐγγινομένη.—*S. Basilii Cæsareæ Archiep.* Op. vol. 1. Paris, 1721. Bened. (In Psalm cxv.)

must the habit of mind which dwelt in the early Church, and was to them as an inward light, be revived in this our day, and still form the qualification to enable men to judge of Bible-inspiration, in this the nineteenth century of the Christian Church. If it shall bring upon us the charge of arguing in a circle, or any other imputation of weakness, we must brave these consequences, and hold to the principle just avowed, and be permitted to remind the theological "critics" of this generation, of the remark of one who thought out all such matters with an independent mind, that 'we are under an intellectual, as well as moral discipline, in this world.' It is as much our duty to deal candidly with the evidence which is afforded us upon subjects which do not admit of any other, as it is to "keep the Commandments" of the Decalogue.

The reasonings which belong to such a subject as that which has now been treated, will be appreciated by students in theology, rather than ordinary private Christians. But these, too, are the " sheep of CHRIST, for whom He shed His blood." Left these should be in danger of " taking any hurt or hindrance by reason of" the sophistries which are rife upon the subject of Bible-inspiration, a word of *encouragement* shall be added for their especial sake. Let them [1] "not be shaken in mind, or troubled" by 'objections' upon this mysterious subject. They may not see their way through all these, only because their minds have not been trained to close thought. But [2] "a man may be fully convinced of the truth of a matter, and upon the strongest reasons, and yet not be able to answer all the difficulties which may be raised upon it." They may find tranquillity by asking this simple question, and dwelling upon the answer to it, What

---

[1] 2 Thess. ii. 2.
[2] BISHOP BUTLER: Durham Charge, 1751.

is the *end* which the Scriptures propose and profess to accomplish? It is to [1] "turn" men "from darkness unto light; and from the power of Satan unto GOD." Now, these effects they have most undeniably produced, from the days that they were first heard of as "Scriptures," to the present hour. This work they carry on regularly in the world, by an invisible but most positive energy, which proves them to contain, as instruments, the "seed of GOD," the same work having gone on through, and having survived, the period of the sceptical cavils against Inspiration of the last Century, and going on, upon a great scale, in our own land, and throughout Christendom, at this moment, in quiet defiance of the opposition which a new school of theologians have attempted to revive.

Upon the whole subject, and as a thought for all alike, whether learned or

---

[1] Acts xviii. 10.

282 Inspiration of the Holy Scriptures.

unlettered Christians, What thanks do we owe to GOD, that, for the knowledge that He [1] "hath given to us eternal life" we are not left to uncertainties; to catch our assurance upon a point so infinitely momentous, from the [2] Sibylline leaves of Tradition, or from any merely human testimony: but, that upon considerations the most weighty, and carrying conviction to our judgments, we can rest in the conclusion, that in the Books of the Old and New Testaments which have come down to us, GOD 'hath [3] *written* to us the great things of His Law,' and of His "glorious Gospel."

---

[1] 1 John v. 11.
[2] . . . . "foliis tantum ne carmina manda,
Ne turbata volent rapidis ludibria ventis."
VIRG. *Æn*. vi. 74.
[3] Hos. viii. 12.

www.ingramcontent.com/pod-product-compliance
Lightning Source LLC
Chambersburg PA
CBHW032056220426
43664CB00008B/1016